Any astute and thoughtful African American recognizes that he or she lives in two worlds—the world of his or her ethnicity as well as the world of Euro-American reality. African American Christians, by and large, have always been socially and politically liberal while remaining theologically and biblically conservative.

It is the attempt of Minister Christopher Signil to explore these realities in the context of an African American response to race, faith, and politics. He has accepted this challenge and makes bold analogies in his investigation of this inquiry. This is a work well worth reading.

—Dr. Charles E. Booth
Mt. Olivet Baptist Church
Columbus, Ohio

To: Sharon Goldsmith
God Bless You !!

RACE,
FAITH, AND
POLITICS

CHRISTOPHER SIGNIL

1 John Six

CREATION
HOUSE

RACE, FAITH, AND POLITICS: 7 QUESTIONS EVERY AFRICAN AMERICAN
CHRISTIAN MUST ANSWER
by Christopher Signil
Published by Creation House
A Charisma Media Company
600 Rinehart Road
Lake Mary, Florida 32746
www.charismamedia.com

Unless otherwise noted, all Scripture quotations are from the King James
Version of the Bible.

Scripture quotations marked NIV are from the Holy Bible, New
International Version. Copyright © 1973, 1978, 1984, 2010, 2011,
International Bible Society. Used by permission.

Scripture quotations marked CJB are from The Complete Jewish Bible,
copyright © 1998 by Jewish New Testament Publications, Inc. Used by
permission.

Design Director: Bill Johnson
Cover design by Nathan Morgan

Visit the author's website: www.racefaithandpolitics.com

Library of Congress Cataloging-in-Publication Data: 2012946649
International Standard Book Number: 978-1-62136-093-3
E-book International Standard Book Number: 978-1-62136-094-0

While the author has made every effort to provide accurate telephone
numbers and Internet addresses at the time of publication, neither the
publisher nor the author assumes any responsibility for errors or for
changes that occur after publication.

First edition

12 13 14 15 16 — 9 8 7 6 5 4 3 2 1
Printed in Canada

DEDICATION

I dedicate this study to my parents, Bishop Willie and Pastor Christine Signil. Mom and Dad, you are indeed the foundation upon which each of my life's endeavors is established. Thank you for demonstrating to me the necessity of making faith and family a priority in all aspects of my life.

Mom, thank you for teaching me to "watch as well as pray," "healing is the children's bread," and for declaring to me, "that I can do all things through Christ." Thank you Mom for displaying to me the true character, compassion, and passion of being a Christian in both word and deed.

Dad, thank you for teaching me "Manners, Respect and Courtesy," and for instilling in me through your words and deeds to, "not be ashamed of the gospel..." and, "they that know their God, shall be strong and do exploits."

I also dedicate this work to my siblings: my brother Willie (Tiger) and his family; my sister Catherine (Cathy) and her family; and my brother Rashawn and his family. I love all of you dearly in a way that words can never describe. To my nieces and nephews: Sinoda, Willie, Lordess, Unique, Melvin, Solomon, and the latest addition, Grace'C, your Uncle Chris loves each of you! Thank you to all of my extended family in the Parks and Signil clan for your love and encouragement!

Acknowledgments

Thank you to every pastor and spiritual leader who I have served under for providing me with a sound example both up close and from a distance of true character, integrity, excellence, and faithfulness in ministry. Thank you to my professors in the Department of Political Science at Virginia State University for your many years of wisdom, intellect, and concern in teaching politics to me and countless others in this generation. Thank you for your commitment in training us to be disciplined and well-informed scholars.

Thank you to Stuart Horowitz of Book Architecture and Ed Cyzewski for your assistance in helping to edit this project and providing valuable feedback, at various stages of its development.

TABLE OF CONTENTS

SECTION III The New Direction

Question 7

POINTS OF REFLECTION

WHILE THIS STUDY consists of seven general questions, throughout each chapter I ask a series of additional, more specific questions which I label as "Point(s) of Reflection." These points of reflection help to provide context to the larger issue addressed in each chapter, and also provide a survey of various perspectives in systematically analyzing each issue.

QUESTION 1: Are You an African American Christian or a Christian African?

Do I see my faith through the lens of my race, or do I see my race through the lens of my faith?

Are there racially definitive issues?

Should my celebration of race diminish or obscure my faith?

Should my conviction of faith supersede my consciousness of and commitment to race-based issues?

Does one have to suffer neglect because of the other?

Is it possible to both celebrate culture and to respect, honor, and love Christ at the same time?

Should my theological paradigm affect my understanding of race?

Would you approve of Minister Farrakhan or a leader from another religion coming to speak in your church on a social or race-based issue?

Should faith matter internally among African Americans?

Should it matter what the color of the candidate is as long as they adequately address issues?

Should biblical theology affect political ideology?

How do Conservative Christians/Fundamentalists/Evangelicals think socially and politically?

How does Liberal Theology address social and political challenges?

Is the accumulation of wealth in itself evil, or is it wealth in the hands of an evil doer more evil?

How does Black Liberation Theology frame its worldview?

Is it possible for men to be really Black and still feel and identity with the biblical tradition expressed in the Old and New Testaments?

Must Black people be forced to deny their identity in order to embrace the Christian faith?

Is there any relationship at all between the work of God and the activity of the Ghetto?

Do the claims in this (Black Liberation) theology indirectly build what it seeks to destroy?

Does this (Black Liberation) theology speak to the present day Black experience?

How does theology impact political ideology?

What is the proper role of government?

QUESTION 2: Are There Standards That All Christians and/or African Americans Should Adhere to on Election Day?

Is there a biblical and/or racial line that all Christians and/or African Americans should adhere to on Election Day and in regards to politics in general?

Are there African American dogmas or political standards?

QUESTION 3: Poverty: Whose Responsibility Is It; Church, Government, or Individual?

Poverty, end it or control it?

Is poverty the church's responsibility?

Is biblical prosperity an answer to poverty?

Prosperity Theology vs. Social Justice Theology: What is Good News to the Poor?

Was Jesus poor and does He hate the rich?

Was Jesus rich and did He fight against poverty?

Is economic stability or prosperity predestined?

Are some predestined to be poor, while others are predestined to be rich, and others are predestined to be middle class?

Is Poverty the Government's Responsibility?

Poverty from the Left: Is Government the Answer?

Is America a welfare state?

If a $787 billion stimulus can only provide short-term solutions, then is the problem outside of the scope of government intervention?

Should a more long-term approach have been taken?

Was stimulating the economy the answer?

Poverty from the Right: Is too much government the problem?

Can the private sector do a better job than the public?

Fiscally, does compromise reflect an impediment or indicator of convictions?

Self-accountability: Are the impoverished responsible for their own predicament?

Can excellence, diligence, and the accumulation of capital eradicate racism?

Can excellence, diligence, and the accumulation of capital supplant racism?

Are Oprah, Michael Jordan, or President Obama primarily seen as being successful or primarily seen as being African American?

Is it really possible to be college educated and have a bachelors, masters, or doctorate degree and be economically poor?

QUESTION 4: Homosexuality in America: Is African American Synonymous with Gay American?

What role should the government play in sex-related issues?

What does the Bible have to say about homosexuality?

Is there a middle ground on the issue in the church?

Homophobia/Homophobic: What do(es) the word(s) really mean?

How then does the church and government proceed on this issue?

QUESTION 5: Abortion, Who Left the Gate Open? And Should We Work to Close It or Should We Open It Wider?

How many abortions take place annually?

Why is there such a mystery?

Is abortion as serious as other issues?

Should abortion be a political deal breaker?

Activist Supreme Court judges: Did the judges overstep their responsibilities in the court decision (Roe v Wade) or where they merely interpreting the law?

Why the apparent silence in the African American community about abortion?

How does abortion fit into Black political and social history?

Fact or fiction: Genocide, eugenics, and racism are hidden in abortion rights?

What role, if any, should ministers play in supporting abortion rights in America?

Preachers leading the charge on abortion: is this a cause of celebration or shame?

What does the Bible have to say about abortion: support, dissent, or indifference?

When does life begin from a biblical perspective?

So should the gates swing open wider for abortion or should it start to close?

QUESTION 6: HIV/AIDS/STDs:
Where Did They Come From and How Do We Get Rid of Them?

Are HIV/AIDS and STDs in America really that serious?

HIV/AIDS: Where did it come from?

Does poverty lead to increased drug use and increased sexual activity?

Does drug addiction lead to poverty and unhealthy sexual practices?

Does an unhealthy sexual appetite lead to drugs or help to enable poverty?

STDs, where do we go from here: how do we attack the problem?

The political Left initiated the war on poverty; the political Right initiated the war on drugs: who is going to initiate the war on undisciplined sexual behavior to address STDs?

Just say no and Abstinence-only programs: Are they worth the investment?

If the federal government should not teach abstinence-only programs, then should federal government even be involved in the discussion?

At what point if any should the federal government inject some idea of right and wrong (morality) into public policy?

Abstinence-only or abstinence-plus education: the dilemma of comprehensive sex education?

How can one effectively advocate abstinence while distributing condoms?

The Bible says fornication and adultery are sins, yet many people do not adhere to it; what should the church do?

Is the message of abstinence in the church ineffective or untested?

QUESTION 7: Where Do We Go from Here?

INTRODUCTION

Race, Faith, and Politics... Which Way Do We Go?

THEY SAY THE three issues that one should never discuss or debate are race, faith, and politics; but over the past decade it seems as if these are the only things America is talking about. The last two presidential elections have placed issues in regards to race and faith front and center in American politics and culture, and the forecast for 2012 is shaping up to do just about the same. From the killing of Trayvon Martin, to contraception mandates on the Catholic Church. From the teachings of Rev. Jeremiah Wright, to the president's support of same-sex marriages. From healthcare to welfare, voting rights to values voters, jobs to justice, immigration to Israel. From the election of the first African American president, to his challenger in 2012 being a Mormon. Issues regarding race and faith seem now more than ever to have come to the center of discussion in all facets of American society.

My political and social worldview, as with most Americans, is directly related to my cultural and spiritual socialization; and it is the relationship between the cultural and the spiritual—in other words, my race and faith—that raises some serious questions during this time in our country's history for me as well as other African Americans who are born-again Christians. In analyzing the current political and social landscape in America, it would appear that *African American born-again Christians are politically and socially firmly planted in two different worlds that are at war with each other.* Let me explain: politically and culturally what it means to be African American is different and at times conflicts with what it means to be a born-again Christian.

African Americans tend to primarily celebrate political and social themes that involve justice, diversity, and equality; while born-again Christians tend to primarily celebrate political and social themes that involve morality, character, and self-accountability. More often than not, these themes are presented as one versus the other, as opposed to one and the other, with there being deep political and social divisions in America in how these themes are commonly interpreted. Is *morality* the enemy of *diversity*? Should *self-accountability* be at war with *justice and equality*? It has become politically and socially uncommon and inconsistent to speak as aggressively against *injustice* as one would against *moral decay*. However, this is the unique ideological position that African Americans who are born-again Christians are in: having very strong beliefs that intersect themes that are important to the African American community at large and the born-again Christian community at large, with both groups having different voting patterns. To understand the root of this political and social dilemma and the tension it causes, one has to look at the history of African Americans and the core beliefs of born-again Christians. I use my personal background as a case study:

I was born in a working class neighborhood in Philadelphia, Pennsylvania, in the late '70s and raised during the decade of the 1980s. During this decade Philadelphia, like many other cites, was experiencing the after-effects of the turbulent '60s and '70s. One of the many positives to come out of the time period in the African American community was that many Black leaders were emerging in various sectors in society. Wilson Goode was elected as the city's first, and one of the nation's first set of big-city, African American mayors. Willie Williams was appointed the city's first African American police commissioner before later going to Los Angeles. Both of these achievements were products of the activism of the '60s and '70s. In sports the Sixers had the best player in the NBA, Julius "Dr. J" Erving; and the Eagles had one of the very few African American starting quarterbacks in the NFL, Randall Cunningham. In addition, the city has always been characterized by its various ethnic communities and strong celebrations of cultural pride. This celebration has been expressed in cultural festivals, block parties, music, and an overall attitude of appreciation for the African American Culture as well as several other ethnicities throughout the city. As a young man growing up in the city, I developed a great sense of appreciation, respect, and love for my culture.

Also, in framing my cultural perspective, I was taught to love, respect, and build relationships with other cultures. I remember during my time in elementary school, my brother and I, like many students in the city, were voluntarily bussed from our neighborhood in South Philly to a school in the Greater North East. This was part of the public school systems' desegregation program, a direct product of the Civil Rights activism of the '60s. This part of the city was far more affluent and had a very large Jewish community, which was much different than the neighborhood in which we lived. During my three years of bussing, I was able to build quality relationships at a young age with individuals who were from different backgrounds than me. These relationships reinforced the ideals I was taught at home: that it was possible to both love and appreciate your culture while respecting and building relationships with people from other cultures. In my experience, one did not have to suffer for the other. After graduating from the Philadelphia Public School system, I attended Virginia State University (VSU), qualified under Historically Black College and Universities (HBCU), in Petersburg, Virginia. Many HBCUs pride themselves in offering a challenging holistic curriculum in an environment where the importance of culture is seen in various facets of formal education.

While my cultural rearing and experiences were indeed valuable and significant in framing my attitudes and beliefs, there was another perspective that was equally as important in framing my political and social worldview: faith!

Faith has always been a major component of my family's life. For as long as I can remember, my mother and father have always been involved in ministry on some level with both of them serving as full-time pastors for over thirty years. As preachers' kids (PKs), my siblings and I have naturally always found ourselves active in some component of ministry from our youth, continuing until this present day. When we were growing up, our faith was characterized by having a relationship with Jesus. Christianity for us was more than just going to church on Sunday morning and Tuesday night (which we rarely ever missed). Our faith was built on striving to display the character, ethics, and actions of Christ in our lives. Our local church consisted primarily of an African American congregation with some Caucasian members. We were officially non-denominational; a choice that was not due to fluctuating positions on doctrinal statements but rather an affirmation of our unity and fellowship with Baptist, Pentecostal, Methodist, and other denominations both White and Black. Doctrinally, we were Charismatic-Pentecostal. Our services were characterized by preaching, teaching, dancing, and singing; but we would fellowship with churches whose expression of worship was not as charismatic as ours.

The Bible for us was a book that was divinely inspired and well respected in our home. To us it represented a book of edification, comfort, ethics, values, *facts*, history, encouragement, redemption, salvation, and most importantly, love. My spiritual formation was also impacted by my extended family, which included cousins, aunts, uncles, and grand-parents. Many of them, in some way or another, were actively involved in ministry as pastors, Sunday school teachers, leaders of neighbor-hood youth Bible studies, women's ministries, campus ministries, music leaders, etc. Faith in God and living a Christian lifestyle was and is a common thread throughout my family. Being a Christian did not mean that everybody always lived a perfect life, but rather everyone through the grace of God strived to embody God's character and values.

My faith was also extended and framed by formal Christian education. In the years immediately before and after participating in the desegrega-tion program, my siblings and I went to Christian schools. My parents made the decision that during our formative years they wanted a part of our education to mirror the values and culture that were taught at home. It always amazes me: some people don't think Christians should go to Christian school on the grounds that it gives them a limited or jaded view of life and faith, and others don't think that Blacks should go to Black colleges on the grounds that it does not mirror a holistic view of society. But as a product of African American, Christian, public, home, and interracial schools from kindergarten through graduate school, I understand that while education should involve a global or holistic expe-rience, it also should involve values and ethics that mirror what is being taught in the home.

So as I reflect on my cultural and spiritual upbringing and values, which were framed while growing up in both an African American and born-again Christian environment, in this environment I devel-oped a love for Christ, a love for culture, and a love for country. Then relating my experiences to the current political and social environment, I came up with seven pertinent questions that needed to be systemati-cally addressed, analyzing how race and faith influence political deci-sion-making and social beliefs.

The study is broken down into three sections: the first section ana-lyzes The Dilemma historically, theologically, culturally, and politically. The second section, called The Deal Breakers, qualitatively analyzes four issues of great significance in our society through the lens of race and faith. The review of the four issues will filter into the final section of the study, The New Direction. In this section I develop a model of political participation for African American born-again Christian voters where both race-based and faith-based concerns are balanced and one does not suffer because of the other.

SECTION I
THE DILEMMA

Question 1

ARE YOU AN
AFRICAN AMERICAN CHRISTIAN OR
A CHRISTIAN AFRICAN AMERICAN?

To some there is no distinction between these two terms, to others the answer to this question is the determining factor in establishing a political philosophy. Still for others the challenge in reconciling race and faith in politics is the main reason for complete and total political apathy. To help with the reconciliation between race and faith, the following question must be considered:

☛ **Point of Reflection:**

Do I see my faith through the lens of my race, or do I see my race through the lens of my faith?

Implicit in the distinction between the concepts *African American Christians* and *Christian African Americans* is the idea that being African American and being Christian represent two different and often conflicting political and social perspectives. While many would vehemently disagree with this statement, voting trends indicate that African Americans at large vote differently than born-again Christians at large.[1] So this begs the question: Is being Christian the antithesis of being African American or vice versa in the political and social arena? The obvious answer to this question is "no." However, this is one of the key distinctions that political strategists and marketing firms build their success on. Let's use the 2000 presidential election as an example: Governor George W. Bush ran a campaign based on morality and character, which was an obvious appeal to faith; Vice President Al Gore said if he was elected the first thing he would do is sign an executive amendment on racial profiling, which was an obvious appeal to race. On a broader level, social and Christian Conservatives are main constituencies of the

Republican Party, while African Americans are a main constituency of the Democratic Party,[2] with both groups having strong negative attitudes about the other. It is almost as if you have to completely abandon one for the other in the political and social arena. Very rarely, if ever, will a campaign attempt to overtly reach out to both African American and Christian voters, and it would appear that a social and political dilemma has been created for African American born-again Christian voters in bringing attitudes and beliefs associated with race and faith over into politics, culture, and various issues in the generation.

Biblically and Racially Definitive and Indifferent Issues

Before I go any further I must make the distinction between the different types of political issues as they relate to faith and race.

Biblically indifferent issues

First, there are biblically indifferent issues; some may use the term *biblically neutral* issues. These are the issues where the Bible does not take a pro or con position. This is not indifferent in substance, but rather indifferent in approach and method. Now some would argue that there are no biblically indifferent issues. However, there is a difference in what the Bible teaches on issues such as term limits for elected officials, campaign finance, and how to properly fund and administer education versus issues such as poverty.

Differences in voting trends among Christians are not a problem when the disparities result from issues that are indeed significant but can be considered biblically indifferent. Examples include disparities on issues that would affect people in various geographical areas differently, whether to have "at large" or district representation; or disparities about symbolic issues such as who should a building be named after, which naval base gets closed down; or even more challenging issues like school vouchers, gun control, etc. These issues will cause differences of opinions and obviously different decisions on Election Day; but I do not see a problem here because positions on either side of these issues do not violate Scripture.

I do not believe that by virtue of the fact that the Bible does not take a pro or con position on each of the *present day issues* that policy framers, political advisors, and cable news networks tell us are significant, it takes anything away from the significance of Scripture in the political and social arena. The Bible was not intended to be a stringent book of do's and don'ts, but rather, a book that provides boundaries for all to live in as they zealously pursue their God-given purpose. There are some positions on certain issues that go outside of those biblical boundaries; however, there are a wide variety of positions on issues that fall within those boundaries and open and honest debate can and should take place.

Biblically definitive issues

The second set of issues I label as biblically definitive issues. For the sake of this study, these are issues that speak directly to foundational biblical beliefs. A position either for or against one of these issues is directly dealt with in Scripture. In no way am I suggesting that *biblically definitive* issues are more important than *biblically indifferent* issues, but rather that there are some things that the Bible speaks clearly to and that there are other issues where Scripture does not speak in the same definitive tone. The second portion of this book, The Deal Breakers, systematically addresses what I would consider some of the biblically definitive issues.

☛ **Point of Reflection:**

　　Are there racially definitive issues?

This dynamic of indifferent and definitive does not play out in the African American community because there is no guiding book or moral document that determines what is and isn't Black. As we will see later in the study (Question 2), each generation faces different challenges and responds to these challenges from their generational, geographical, and economic perspectives; so it is difficult to find issues where we can say conclusively that every Black is morally or culturally bound to support. With that being said, there are some issues that have been the catalyst for advancements and massive achievements in the African American community, and the costs should be weighed before these issues are discarded.

The dilemma that is presented exclusively in the African American community is the race-faith dynamic. This dilemma is created because there are two growing factions in the African American community. One faction openly and proudly celebrates race while at the same time diminishing and discouraging the necessity of faith and church. This group sees faith, or what they may label as organized religion such as Christianity, as an impediment to the African American community. In this view faith is more of a submissive and manipulative element, while race is seen as a more dominate variable in outlining beliefs and attitudes.

The other faction sees faith as being the more dominant or controlling variable, and that any definition or understanding of race and culture should be channeled through our understanding of faith, God, and
religion (I will flesh this debate out in greater detail in the next chapter).
Here faith is seen as being the dominant variable in establishing core
beliefs and values; in other words, a belief, dogma, or attitude associated
with faith can never be compromised or should never take precedence
over race.

☛ **Points of Reflection:**

Should my celebration of race diminish or obscure my faith?

*Should my conviction of faith supersede my consciousness of and
commitment to race-based issues?*

Does one have to suffer neglect because of the other?

*Is it possible to both celebrate culture and to respect, honor, and
love Christ at the same time?*

This race and faith dilemma is best seen by contrasting the attitudes
of many Black Christians in regards to the Million Man March led
by Nation of Islam leader Minister Louis Farrakhan in the mid 1990s
(which ultimately revolved around the acceptance of non-Christian
social leaders in the African American community) with the attitudes of
Black Christians in the early 2000s toward Bishop Carlton Pearson and
his teaching on Universalism.

Bishop Carlton Pearson was in many respects just as influential a
leader in the Protestant church in the early 2000s as arguably anyone
else in America. Bishop Pearson was a trailblazer in terms of the African
American mega-church, mega conferences, and international television programs. He was even an award-winning gospel music artist.
Bishop Pearson was a product of the Church of God in Christ, one of
the largest denominations in America, and a spiritual son/mentee of
renowned evangelist Oral Roberts. In the early 2000s, Bishop Pearson
began to preach the doctrines of Universalism and relativism which
were antithetical to the movement that he came from. The doctrine of
inclusion that he embraced categorically challenged some of the major
tenets of Orthodox Christian doctrine for which he once advocated. As
a result of his change, he was labeled by a group of African American
church leaders a "heretic" and unofficially excommunicated from many
Christian circles. He eventually would lose his church and the respect

of many African American Christians, primarily and almost exclusively due to his embracing Universalism. In other words, this position by the church was an indicator of its strong commitment to a theological stance and a willingness to stand firm on fundamental beliefs despite race.

The reverse happened in 1995 when Nation of Islam leader and activist Louis Farrakhan, along with several other prominent social leaders, organized a rally at the nation's capital targeted at Black men. The goal of this event was to target a series of social issues facing African American men. One of the subthemes of the march was "A Day of Atonement." This was a call for unity and a charge for African American men to refocus on their personal and spiritual priorities. This historic event, which attracted hundreds of thousands of African American men from around the country, was a day of fellowship, unity, and renewal. However, this event was led by the leader of the Nation of Islam, a religious organization whose beliefs are just as antithetical to Orthodox Christianity as Universalism. Nevertheless, this event and Minister Farrakhan have not been excommunicated in the same manner that Bishop Pearson has, which would indicate that a commitment to race transcends theological differences, which was not the case with Bishop Pearson.

☛ **Point of Reflection:**

Should my theological paradigm affect my understanding of race?

As we will discover later in this chapter, there are a wide variety of beliefs that fall under the wider umbrella of Christianity. However, most African American Christians would consider themselves to be theologically Orthodox or Fundamentalist, viewpoints which hinge on the belief that Jesus is the only way to salvation, peace, and atonement. To some, staying away from an event such as the Million Man March purely based upon strong religious differences is considered bigotry; but to others the concern is the absence of the necessity of Jesus Christ in addressing the challenges facing African American men.

☛ **Points of Reflection:**

Would you approve of Minister Farrakhan or a leader from another religion coming to speak in your church on a social or race-based issue?

Should faith matter internally among African Americans?

Let's examine two sets of competing factors that may explain why there is an apparent inconsistency in balancing race and faith in politics and culture among African American born–again Christians. The first set of factors emphasizes and/or de-emphasizes race and/or faith in politics. The second set of factors is purely theological in nature and can be determined based upon how Scripture is interpreted and then used and applied to politics. What we will find from this example is a unique dilemma that impacts African American Christian voters.

Deracialization and De-Faithization

Deracialization

Since 1900, there have been a total of three elected African American United States senators, two elected governors, and one president; a total of five elected African Americans in the highest office in state and federal government, with President Obama being elected as a senator and later president. Of these five elected officials, the majority of them have run campaigns that have neutralized race-related issues and have strategically distanced themselves from most major discussion of race on the campaign trail. Throughout much of their campaigns, the candidates spoke very little about issues that were directly race specific and tended to focus more on issues that transcended race or had more of a mass appeal. One of the greatest examples of deracialization is the 2008 presidential campaign of Barack Obama.

During the election cycle, Senator Obama ran a campaign with the themes of "Hope" and "Change We Can Believe In." This change and hope he advocated was change in healthcare, foreign affairs, and the economy; but for the vast majority of his campaign, he avoided as often as possible the "elephant in the room," which was race. His campaign team did everything that they could to keep race out, while others did everything that they could to keep race in. His campaign dealt with race only when they were politically forced to do so. Such was the case on Tuesday, March 18, 2008, in Philadelphia when he delivered his speech on race from Constitutional Hall. This speech, which was his first overt discussion of race during the campaign, was given when he was experiencing massive criticism based upon his relationship with Rev. Jeremiah A. Wright. In the speech Senator Obama stated:

> Throughout the first year of this campaign, against all predictions to the contrary, we saw how hungry the American people were for

this message of unity. Despite the temptation to view my candidacy through a purely racial lens, we won commanding victories in states with some of the whitest population in the country. In South Carolina, where the Confederate Flag still flies, we built a powerful coalition of African Americans and white Americans.[3]

Senator Obama did not base his campaign on race-related issues, such as affirmative action, racial profiling, and reparations; nor did he present himself as "standing on the shoulders" of Martin Luther King Jr., Malcolm X, or Marcus Garvey. Instead he focused on race-neutral issues and images that had more of a mass appeal. He consistently played the middle ground even in his support of Rev. Wright and in his critique of race relations.

> I can no more disown him [Rev. Wright] than I can disown the Black community. I can no more disown him than I can my White grandmother—a woman who helped raise me, a woman who sacrificed again and again for me, a woman who loves me as much as she loves anything in this world, but a woman who once confessed her fear of Black men who passed by her on the street, and who on more than one occasion has uttered racial or ethnic stereotypes that made me cringe.[4]

Senator Obama's deracialization was the part of his campaign strategy that frustrated some of the elder voices from the Civil Rights era and some of the current African American political leaders; this was part of what arguably led to some of their very passive support and in some cases lack of support during the Democratic Primary in 2008. However, despite their criticism and passivity, from a strategic perspective he understood that if his goal was to actually win the presidency, then this is the route he had to take in building a campaign that had more of a mass appeal. This was a different approach than some of the African Americans who had previously sought the presidency. Even after his election, President Obama has continued on somewhat of a deracialized path, and has arguably distanced himself from race-based politics. Through his actions he has arguably tried not to define himself as a "Black president," but as the president of all; he has played middle of the road on race relations, even to a fault; this was seen in his Administration's response to two high-profile race-based situations that occurred during his first Administration.

Early in his Administration he was vocally critical of the officers who arrested African American Harvard University Professor Henry Gates as

Gates was entering his own home. The arrest was due to mistaken identity, with the arrest being viewed as alleged "racial profiling." The president would go on and apologize for his comments against the officers, and he would later bring the professor and the arresting officer to the White House for lunch. The following year the president's Administration forced the resignation of Shirley Sherrod, an African American State Director with the United States Department of Agriculture, based upon comments by her that were taken out of context and seen as racist, largely fueled by some in the media. When the full video of Shirley Sherrod's speech was seen, the president offered an apology to her and offered her another position in the government. What we find overall from both situations is the president attempting to be balanced on issues regarding race. The response by the media and general public discourse about both events reveal that race is still a very sensitive subject in America. While there are many criticisms with the position of avoiding direct discussions and appeals on race, in our current racially sensitive culture, some have chosen to minimize or not address race-based issues in order to allegedly keep the peace.

Deracialization is a tactic that is typically used by African Americans from the Right and/or African Americans seeking statewide or federal offices. I heard a preacher once say, "God does not see race, so neither should we." While the statement was made in good faith, this statement does not capture the biblical position on race. All throughout the Bible there were distinctions made on race, but ultimately there was not deference to one race over another.

☛ **Point of Reflection:**

Should it matter what the color of the candidate is as long as they adequately address issues?

While some tend to deemphasize race in politics, others tend to deemphasize faith in an attempt to gain mass appeal.

De-faithization

African Americans have seen significantly greater success in electoral politics on the local level. Each of the top five Metropolitan Statistical Areas in the United States has had at least one Black mayor and many Black city councilmen in the past twenty years. One of the factors leading to higher success rates on the state and local levels is that most of these areas are predominantly African American. In some cases the media and the campaigns have focused directly on race-related issues, while strategically deemphasizing references, analogies, and direct appeals to faith or faith-based issues.

One of the trends that has taken place in recent years is the scope of civil rights, civil liberties, diversity, and inclusion has immensely increased. In the past, these were political code words targeted to ethnic minorities. Now the meaning of these terms and ideas has broadened to include the pro-choice movement, the gay rights movement, the staunch separation of church and state ideology, and the entitlement movement. To appeal to this group, candidates have systematically backed off of rhetoric, ideas, issues, and references to church and Bible in order to attract support from this growing demographic. The merger of these groups was evident in the strong feelings of betrayal that some gay Americans had in California toward African Americans who voted in favor of Proposition 8 in 2008.[5] It was the feeling that African Americans turned their back on their progressive partners in the election.

What is ironic about de-faithization is that while most of the campaigning in various state and local campaigns is done in churches, there are some issues that can be considered faith-based issues that do not get brought up in these elections. Some will use the church for campaigning, community organizing, and community outreach, yet will condemn the church when the church takes a firm stand on an issue that may not be socially or politically correct. Some may counter that the idea of de-faithization is rooted in a narrow interpretation of Scripture held by those who systematically avoid social justice. While there may be some validity to this position, it is also quite possible that when Scripture and faith are seen through the lens of one's preestablished political ideology, its scope is limited to certain issues in order to attract a massive following.

Those on the Left have taken the position that we believe in Scripture but we leave it at the door when it comes to politics; while those on the Right tend to be more overt in their presentation of Scripture, while very passive on addressing race-based issues or celebrating diversity.

Similar to deracialization, regardless of one's position on the de-emphasis of faith, de-faithization has proven to be an effective method of campaigning in some races. The minimizing or emphasis of race and/or faith is a factor to some in determining preferences for political participation and in determining whether one is an African American Christian or Christian African American. To some the issue is purely theological.

☛ **Point of Reflection:**

Should biblical theology affect political ideology?

To many, one's interpretation of the Bible is where all distinctions begin and end. What is very encouraging is that although the variances in biblical ideology are vast, both sides of the political spectrum still value having a position validated by Scripture. While this respect and deference to the Bible by the majority on the Left and Right offers optimism to believers in the Bible, concern still remains that some individuals/groups will not go to Scripture in search of truth but will rather go to Scripture to create or validate their truth. One has to wonder if it is better to leave the Bible completely out of the political and social equation, rather than bring it in and manipulate its meaning.

While the methods of interpretation and theological perspectives are very fragmented, let's explore two of the main theological perspectives,[6] Conservative and Liberal Theology, and then two other prominent theologies in the twentieth century. It should become clear how each perspective is very different and how each frames their political and social worldview.

Liberal and Conservative Theology

☛ **Point of Reflection:**

How do Conservative Christians/Fundamentalists/Evangelicals think socially and politically?

For the purposes of this study, these terms will be used interchangeably in describing traditional theology. There are indeed some legitimate distinctions between those who use these different terms. However, for the most part these terms represent in varying degrees the more classic or standard Protestant Theology in America.

Protestant Theology draws its roots from the Lutheran Reformation of the sixteenth century. As the name infers, Protestantism was a "protest" against ideas and beliefs purported by the Catholic Church.[7] From the sixteenth century to our present culture there have been countless variations and denominations under the broader umbrella of Protestantism. There are many variations, but for the most part the Conservative or Orthodox faction of Protestantism adheres to the following five core beliefs, as originally developed by the General Assembly of the Presbyterian Church in

1910. The beliefs are known as the Doctrinal Deliverance of 1910 or the Five Fundamentals.[8]

1. **Scripture is Inerrant and God Inspired**: This is the belief that the facts, events, and ideas that are recorded in Scripture are historically factual and without error in their original written form. In addition, the thoughts and ideas of Scripture originated with God and not with man. Hence, Scripture and its ideas about culture and society are rooted in absolute truth. This belief strongly challenges the notion carried by other ideologies that one can stand on and trust in beliefs that they believe are merely mythical, literary, or metaphoric. The inerrancy of Scripture means that the social ethics and mores espoused by the Bible are indeed divine in nature and should not be compromised based upon the nuances of each generation. In this view, ethics and truth are absolute.

2. **The Virgin Birth of Jesus**: Orthodox Theology holds that Jesus was fully God and at the same time fully man. This belief hinges on the understanding that Jesus' mother, Mary, was a virgin at the time of Jesus' conception and she was divinely impregnated by the Holy Spirit.[9] While other theological persuasions will assent to this belief metaphorically, the literal truth of the virgin birth is one of the two attributes of Jesus' life that distinguishes Him from any other man and establishes His divinity, along with His humanity. This fact gives His message greater authority than any other political, religious, or social leader that has existed before or after Him.

3. **Christ Died as an Atonement for Sins**: The sin factor in society is a key component of Conservative Theology and places the death, burial, and resurrection of Jesus Christ at the core of the belief system. The death of Jesus was His sacrifice for the sins of man. Why is there crime, hatred, racism, bigotry, and oppression? The core of all of these evils according to Conservative Theology is sin, which is prevalent in society. Because man is evil in nature and on his own lacks the ability to do good, Jesus died as an atonement for man's sins. Conservative Theology teaches that Jesus is the only mediatory between God and humanity to redeem all people from their sins. Put simply, the world has a problem called sin, and Jesus' atoning work on Calvary was and is the answer to that problem.

4. **The Bodily Resurrection of Jesus**: The belief in the literal bodily resurrection from the dead of Jesus illustrates His superiority over life and death and His victory in redeeming man from sin. According to Orthodox Theology, it is through belief and faith in His death, burial, and most importantly His resurrection that man is redeemed and justified

from sin and evil. Man through his good works, moral actions, and positive ethics cannot redeem himself or society from sin.

5. **Literal and Historical Accuracy of Christ Performing Miracles**: Christ's divine power was used to bring hope, healing, and redemption to many during His lifetime. These various acts by Christ illustrate His compassion and concerns for the destitute and His ability to meet their needs.

(Although not included in the five fundamentals, there is a sixth attribute of Orthodox Theology that is commonly believed, and is essential to this belief system.)

6. **Heavenly Hope (Ultimate Justice/Justification)**: The hope of Christianity is the belief that when earthly life ends, there is life after death, in that the believer will spend eternity in comfort and paradise with Jesus.[10] Other theologies have argued that with the Fundamentalist position of life after death and the blessed hope of spending eternity with Jesus, some have taken their attention off of current acts of injustice, poverty, and evils in society and have sat lethargically waiting on their "mansion" in the sky.[11]

From an Orthodox perspective, heavenly hope does not validate or indirectly precipitate present injustices and evils in society. Heavenly hope gives hope and comfort to the believer.[12] In other words, there is an expectation that on earth men are to "do justly [fight for justice], and to love mercy, and to walk humbly with thy God."[13] In other words, men are to work aggressively for justice and peace in our present world; but there is also an equal understanding that earth is not the end, and there is ultimate justification and redemption in spending eternity with God.

For many years these beliefs stood as the core of all Protestant Theology. However, as various cultural and spiritual influences began to rise, along with various social changes and an increase in the authority of science and reason, these beliefs were viewed by *some* as not adequately dealing with the needs of each generation and not satisfying the laws of science, reason, and logic. As a result, a series of shifts began to take place by some in Protestantism from faith to reason to relativism. Below I outline the major theological positions of the last century in shaping thought and framing social, political, and ethical ideologies.

Each of the sets of beliefs stated below are in essence a response to Orthodox Theology in varying degrees. While there is disagreement among the positions below on several matters of theology, each of the sets of beliefs are together in their position of having a great disdain for Orthodox Theology.

☛ **Point of Reflection:**

How does Liberal Theology address social and political challenges?

Liberal Theology is rooted in the idea that God is revealed through an alleged intelligent, rational inquiry into Scripture which is rooted *exclusively* in reason and discounts the miraculous. This inquiry into Scripture cannot take place without taking into account the historical, philosophical, and social climate of the interpreter of revelation. This method of inquiry makes the process entirely subjective and makes the Bible a fallible document that must exclusively be viewed in the historical context of the authors.[14] Henry P. Van Dusen, who was the former president of Union Theological Seminary in New York City, which can be considered the Mecca of Liberal Theology in America, argues in his book *The Vindication of Liberal Theology* that Christianity has evolved from various traditions such as "Hebrew Religion and Greek Philosophy," then later "when it came to the Greco-Roman world." One of the chief concerns of the faith was to make it socially relevant, which according to Van Dusen is the essence and roots of Liberal Theology.[15] He further explains that the "central intellectual motive of Liberal Theology is to make the Christian faith intelligible and credible, comprehensive and convincing to intelligent, informed honest minds of each successive era."[16]

This theology encouraged the reliance on truth as a product of cultural relativity that could not be characterized by definitive statements and creeds but rather progressive propositions that sought to speak to the needs of individual generations.

Liberal Theology embraces what has been known as higher textual criticism; this challenges the entire authenticity of Scripture with a sharp critique of the location, date, authorship, and literary genre of the biblical text.[17] In this view, the Bible as a whole is not infallible or God inspired. This view has consistently rejected the miracles and supernatural events in the life of Christ and in Scripture as being valid or as being a necessary component of faith. In addition, with this deference to science, the Bible is not regarded as an ultimate authority but rather one in a series of sources of truth which cannot be viewed as objective or definitive. *In this view, any political or social ideas coming from the Bible cannot be considered as absolute.*

More broadly, Liberal Theology accepts that there is an underlying
continuity in thought that bridges the gap between the Christian faith
and other faiths and gives "tolerance toward other religions, and toward
no religion."[18] Not only did this continuum exist between Christianity
and other faiths, but it also existed between "God and humanity" and
"reason and revelation." [19]

Liberals consider themselves Christocentric, in that there is a significant amount of attention placed on the historical Jesus. While most
Liberal theologians would agree that there was a man named Jesus, He
ministered to the poor and downtrodden and was subsequently cru-
cified,[20] all other details of His life are up for debate. This theology is
absent a literal resurrection and virgin birth, which is at the core of
Orthodox Theology.

According to Van Dusen the connections between the historical Jesus
and the living Jesus are "the words, deeds, mind, spirit, faith of the man
Jesus of Nazareth.... All else is secondary and dubious accretion."[21]

So, already we see two clearly different worldviews in Liberal and
Conservative Theology, it is clear to see that Liberal Theology sees truth
and culture as being relative; here there is no absolute standard of right
or wrong, a consistent questioning of the truth. One of the most noted
and widely influential Liberal theologians of the past century was Walter
Rauschenbusch and his correlation of faith to the social challenges in
the world through a liberal worldview in which he makes a case for the
Social Gospel.

Walter Rauschenbusch and the Social Gospel

The essential purpose of Christianity was to transform human society
into the kingdom of God by regenerating all human relations and
reconstituting them in accordance with the will of God.[22]

Walter Rauschenbusch was pastor of the Second German Baptist
Church in New York City from 1886–1897 and then Professor at Rochester
Seminary in New York City from 1902–1918. Like many other Liberal pastors and theologians, Rauschenbusch was reared in Orthodox Theology,
but believed that the teachings and practices of Orthodox Theology did
not effectively deal with the social and cultural issues that were facing
his generation. Rauschenbusch's attempt to make Scripture relevant
to the needs of society resulted in the Social Gospel. The focus of the
Social Gospel according to Rauschenbusch is "any teaching on the sinful

condition of the race and on its redemption from evil which fails to do justice to the social factors and processes in sin and redemption must be incomplete, unreal, and misleading."[23]

Rauschenbusch argues that the central message and purpose of Christianity is the expansion and continuation of the kingdom of God, which is expressed in the Social Gospel through the work of social justice. The message of the Social Gospel focuses on the needs, empowerment, and sins of society at large as opposed to individuals. This theology teaches that God's focus and attention has consistently been toward equality, fairness, justice, and camaraderie in society at large, and firmly against any and all forms of individualism. This includes individualism in sin, salvation, culture, politics, church, and even in conceptions of God.

Here, Rauschenbusch argues, "The conception of God held by a social group is a social product. Even if it originated in the mind of a solitary thinker or prophet, as soon as it becomes the property of a social group, it takes on the qualities of that group."[24] In other words, according to this belief, God and Jesus can become a product of man's thought. The Social Gospel favors a move toward democracy in government and in the church and is strongly against capitalism because capitalism is a catalyst for social injustice.[25]

The Social Gospel continues with this theme in that "attention is concentrated on questions of public morality, on wrongs done by whole classes or professions of men, on sins which enervate and submerge entire mill towns or agriculture states. These sins have been side stepped by the old theology [Orthodox]."[26]

On a broader level the Social Gospel tends to attribute sin to the ills in the environment and the community, while placing less responsibility on the individuals.[27] This theology strongly abhors the traditional doctrine of the fall of man,[28] which is at the core of Orthodox Theology, and is an essential element of Christ's atoning work on Calvary.

This doctrine teaches that sin is not biologically transmitted or inherited but rather is socially transmitted, "one generation corrupts the next."[29] This issue lends itself to the deep-rooted rifts between Liberal and Orthodox Theology.

The Social Gospel and Jesus

In terms of Jesus, the Social Gospel is only concerned with Jesus' impact on society and His fight for social justice; according to Rauschenbusch, "his life is what counted; his death was part of it."[30]

Liberal Theology teaches that Jesus' focus on earth was *exclusively* as an advocate for poor people: "He [Jesus] realized a profound danger to the better self in the pursuit of wealth."[31] Rauschenbusch argues that in Jesus' teachings, "the poor as a class are made identical with the meek and godly, and the 'rich' and 'wicked' are almost synonymous terms."[32]

☛ **Points of Reflection:**

Is the accumulation of wealth in itself evil, or is it wealth in the hands of an evil doer more evil?

Liberal Theology vs. Conservative Theology

The tension between these theologians seems to rest between the social and the individual, external and internal, relative and absolute, self-accountability and communal responsibility. Conservatism begins with self and then branches into a communal or social good. Liberalism (the Social Gospel) sees everything from the vantage point of the communal or social responsibility, even at the cost or de-emphasis of self. Conservative Theology makes the born-again believer's personal relationship with Christ, or Christ indwelling in the believer, the starting point for personal redemption (which is necessary), which filters into social and political change. Liberal Theology sees Christ at work in society as essential and in some respects almost exclusive as the essential framework for the gospel. The good of society then is not determined by the beliefs and ideas associated with an omniscient, immutable God, but rather according to the ideas, beliefs, and mores associated from thinking or rational men. The God of Conservatism is infinite. He sees and knows all, whereas the God of Liberalism is finite and a product of man's wisdom.

There is one more quasi-Liberal theologian that we want to explore before relating theology to political ideology. This theologian sought to bring liberal ideas to African Americans in the 1960s and his theology had a major impact on the 2008 Presidential election.

☛ **Point of Reflection:**

How does Black Liberation Theology frame its worldview?

James Cone and Black Liberation Theology

The 2008 Presidential election was almost dominated by stories surrounding the views of Barack Obama's pastor, the Rev. Jeremiah Wright. Rev. Wright served as pastor of the Trinity United Church of Christ in Chicago, Illinois, a church that sees and celebrates Christ through the vantage point of a Liberal African/African American tradition. The motto of the church is "Unashamedly Black and Unapologetically Christian"; and much of the teaching of Dr. Wright is rooted in Black Liberation Theology, a theology that gained prominence in the late 1960s in America.

In the mid- to late-1960s there was a growing frustration in the African American community with the previous methods of fighting segregation, a growing militancy among younger African Americans, and a renewed sense of reflection and pride of the African Culture and Pan-Africanism that was perceived as being lost through integration and assimilation into the American culture. While some in the Liberation Generation[33] completely shunned Christianity, others have attempted to build a bridge between Black Nationalism and Christianity, especially in Dr. James Cone's Black Liberation Theology.

Cone argued that Black Liberation Theology grew out of Martin Luther King's paradigm of Christianity and Malcolm X's paradigm or expression of being Black. Cone argued that King's Christianity was void of identity with race and Malcolm's expression of race was void of Christianity. So Black Liberation Theology was a leftward leaning Christian theology for Black Nationalism or militancy.[34]

In his 1969 book, *Black Theology and Black Power,* James Cone raised three important questions:

☞ **Points of Reflection:**

"Is it possible for men to be really Black and still feel and identity with the biblical tradition expressed in the Old and New Testaments?"[35]

"Must Black people be forced to deny their identity in order to embrace the Christian faith?"[36]

"Is there any relationship at all between the work of God and the activity of the Ghetto?"[37]

In dealing with these issues, Dr. Cone explains the correlation between Black Power and Christianity as well as the meaning and necessity of a Black Liberation Theology from the vantage point of an African American who is theologically liberal.

Black Liberation Theology is rooted in the idea that any effective theology must be for those who are "humiliated and abused."[38] Much of this theology draws its biblical inspiration from the experiences of the Israelites in Egyptian captivity.[39] This theology draws a distinction between Blacks as the oppressed and Whites as the oppressors, with God's position as being either for Blacks (the oppressed) or for Whites (the oppressors), but not for both.[40] Dr. Cone argues that there is an inherent evil in Whites. He states, "Black Theology seeks to analyze the satanic nature of whiteness and the need for liberation."[41] He further states, "American White Theology is a theology of the antichrist...placing God's approval on White oppression of Black existence."[42] According to Dr. Cone, White Theology "has not been involved with Black Liberation. It has been basically a theology of the White oppressor, giving religious sanction to the genocide of Amerindians and the enslavement of Africans."[43] According to Dr. Cone, "The appearance of Black Theology on the American scene then is due to the failure of White religionist to relate the Gospel of Jesus to the pain of being Black in a White racist society."[44] While Dr. Cone does argue that Blacks are not the only disadvantaged group in America, this theology does make an existential claim that "God is at work in the Black community, vindicating Black victims of White oppression."[45] Cone attempts to use Blackness as a symbol of oppression on a larger scale in America.[46]

☛ **Point of Reflection:**

> *Do the claims in this theology indirectly build what it seeks to destroy?*

Black Liberation Theology echoes the Social Gospel in taking emphasis away from justice and redemption in heaven and placing emphasis almost exclusively on justice on earth.[47] This theology ultimately accepts many of the higher textual criticisms, strongly abhors many of the core tenets of Orthodox Theology, and only sees religious or scriptural authority as it relates to the "Black demand for freedom Now,"[48] this theology accepts "any religious idea which exalts Black dignity and creates a restless drive for freedom."[49]

Black Liberation Theology and Jesus!

This theology teaches that for Jesus to have any relevance to the Black experience in America, which Dr. Cone defines as oppressive, Jesus

Himself must be oppressed or "Black."[50]According to Cone, "Being with him (Jesus) is dependent on his being with us in the oppressed Black condition."[51] A Black Jesus is necessary in explaining that the living Jesus is an active force in the fight for liberation and in "threatening the structure of evil."[52] According to Dr. Cone, the concept of a Black Jesus is not concerned with Jesus being Black in a literal sense, but rather in a sense of making Christ relevant to the current Black experience and showing Jesus as the oppressed and as a symbol of liberation.[53]

☛ **Point of Reflection:**

   Does this theology speak to the present day Black experience?

The Social Impact of Walter Rauschenbusch and James Cone

Rauschenbusch and Cone had a significant following, and in the decades following Rauschenbusch's death, their theological legacy had a major impact across the country and around the world. Cone's legacy was seen in the national exposure that his ideas received during the 2008 presidential election, and the fact that nearly every major African American seminary in America bases its doctrine on Black Liberation Theology. In the case of Rauschenbusch, his first book, *Christianity and the Social Crisis,* was written in 1907. Now, over a full century later, many major liberal and quasi-liberal denominations in America and many Liberal theologians cite his ideas and theology of social justice as their primary source of reference. Arguably, the entire Civil Rights movement was rooted in Rauschenbusch's Social Gospel. In addition, Reinhold Niebuhr, Martin Luther King Jr., Desmond Tutu, many United States presidents, and most of the prominent Civil Rights activist have cited his work as an inspiration and motivating force behind their ministry or work.

   For the most part, Liberal and quasi-Liberal theologians can accept most of the ideas of Rauschenbusch and Cone, while a Conservative theologian finds many challenges with most of their claims and only sees the differences between the two men as marginal. What we have are clear and legitimate differences in worldviews and in the understanding of God, man, justice, and redemption. Now we turn to how these sets of beliefs are seen in voting trends.

Application of Theology in Voting Trends

One of the interesting trends when dealing with race, politics, and faith is the distinction and correlation between these three variables when it comes to voting or, more specifically, answering this question:

☛ **Point of Reflection:**

How does theology impact political ideology?

In predominately White congregations (this includes both the White theologically Liberal and theologically Conservative), there is more of a direct correlation between theology and political ideology as reflected in voting trends. According to a recent study by the Barna research groups, White Christians voted largely for Sen. McCain in 2008 by a margin of 73 percent to 26 percent, whereas White non-Christians voted largely for Sen. Obama by a margin of 56 percent to 39 percent.[54] A study by the Pew Research Poll in 2012 found that those with a more leftward-leaning social ideology tend to vote for Democrats, with the Democratic party becoming "more secular," [55] which I would define as aligning more closely with a Liberal Theology. A 2005 study by the Pew Research group found that "Americans who regularly attend worship services, and hold traditional religious views increasingly vote Republican, while those who are less connected to religious institutions, and more secular in their outlook tend to vote Democrat."[56] So what we have in our current political climate is a direct correlation with Caucasians between theology and political ideology. Those with a more Conservative Theology tend to vote socially conservative, while those with a more Liberal Theology tend to vote socially liberal. This suggests that theology is a controlling variable for Caucasian Christians voting trends. However, with African Americans the relationship between race and theology (or faith) in voting trends is not as direct.

The Dynamic of Shifting Theological Priorities (Ideologies)

In the African American community there is more of an indirect cor-relation between theology and political ideology, or what I label as the dynamic of shifting theological priorities (ideologies), which indicates that the controlling variable for African American Christians is not the-ology. This dynamic is the practice of having one theological perspective on a personal level and another on a public or political level. According to The Barna Group's 2008 presidential election exit polls, "There were no statistically significant differences between Black born-again voters and Black non-born-again voters."[57] Historian Mark Noll calls this recurring dynamic "a cooperation in the African American community between theological Liberals (who tended to picture the work of God in mythic terms) and theological Conservatives (who saw the work of God in intensely realistic terms) for the purpose of advancing social goals."[58] In 2009 a Gallop Poll indicated that there was no difference between voting trends of highly religious and not religious African Americans, with each strongly supporting Democrats.[59]

This dynamic is key to understanding African American Christian voting trends and political participation at large. According to a 2009 study conducted by the PEW Research Group, "African Americans are markedly more religious on a variety of measures than the U.S. population as a whole."[60] This belief ranges from "frequency of prayer and worship service attendance to belief in God."[61] This study also found compared with the population overall, for instance, African Americans are more likely to believe in God with absolute certainty (88 percent vs. 71 percent among the total adult population), interpret Scripture as the literal Word of God (55 percent vs. 33 percent) and express a belief in angels and demons (83 percent vs. 68 percent). They also are more likely to say they are absolutely convinced about the existence of life after death (58 percent vs. 50 percent) and to believe in miracles (84 percent vs. 79 percent).[62]

For example, in many African American Holiness and Pentecostal churches, the primary message from the pulpit focuses more on inward sanctification, strong ethics in personal conduct, traditional views on issues related to sex and sexuality, and strict adherence to scriptural guidelines. This message has been summed up in the ageless phrase "Holiness or Hell." The same applies in many African American Baptist congregations as well. While there are wide distinctions in Baptist theology, many Black Baptists consider themselves Orthodox or Fundamentalist in theology. Supporters of the Fundamentalist position would express their commitments in the common phrase "the Bible said it, I believe it, and that settles it." However, many of the African American proponents of these statements do not display the same level of dogmatism toward faith on Election Day. The focus on Election Day tends to shift to a more external or social holiness, which would involve issues such as poverty, social justice, and race relations, while relaxing some of the sharper rhetoric on internal holiness in regards to politics and popular culture that has become the pillar of much of the doctrine in African American churches.

The PEW study also found that "African-Americans are more likely to describe their political ideology as Conservative (32 percent) or moderate (36 percent) than as Liberal (23 percent)."[63] The same study found that African Americans also express a "high-degree of comfort with religion's role in politics." This position closely resembles White evangelicals.[64] But in the African American Christian community, issues of external holiness seem to trump issues of internal or personal holiness in the context of politics, despite the very strong social and theological views carried by African American Christians. Another Pew study found that race was one of the high factors in determining electoral decisions in the 2000 and 2004 presidential elections at large in America; primarily due to African Americans' very strong support for the Democratic Party that represents socially liberal views.[65]

Based upon the above data, I make the case that *African American born-again Christians are firmly planted in two different worlds, strongly committed to theological Conservatism on a level higher than the Caucasian Christians, and at the same time strongly committed to voting for socially Liberal candidates in one of the highest percentages compared to other races in America.* So let's explore two possibilities as to why this dynamic exists; the first revolves around the inability to specifically distinguish where support and or disagreement lies within a party's larger political platform, and the second involves the larger political and ideological issue regarding the "role of government," which is and has been a key issue in politics.

The Absence of an Electoral Line-Item Veto in Politics

The line-item veto is probably one of the most important budgetary tools in all of politics. This tool gives executives and in some cases legislators the opportunity to support certain pieces of legislation without having to compromise on other pieces that they fundamentally disagree with. In addition, the line-item veto allows quality legislation and issues to stand without being tainted by unnecessary and at times irrelevant legislation better known as "PORK" or "pork-barrel spending." Although this is primarily a budgetary tool, the theory behind the line-item veto on a larger scale is to send a message loud and clear as to what exactly one supports and what one disagrees with. The inability to make a clear distinction between what one supports and what one does not support is one of the factors that explains the apparent dynamic of shifting theological priorities.

Many times issues that are significant to African American born-again Christians are frequently intertwined with issues that African American born-again Christians do not support. As opposed to speaking out against the policies that these voters disagree with, African Americans born-again Christians will speak in favor of what they agree on, while remaining silent on their dissent, thus leaving the perception of support for the entire package. An example is with the purpose statement of the National Organization of Women (NOW). Here is part of their purpose statement:

> NOW stands against all oppression, recognizing that racism, sexism and homophobia are interrelated, and that other forms of oppression such as classism and ableism work together with these three to keep power and privilege concentrated in the hands of a few. [66]

While this is a subject that I deal with in greater detail in Question 6, many have an issue with intertwining the scope and goals of women's rights, racism, and gay and lesbian rights without making proper distinctions with the manner in which some of these terms are used and have sent a message of support for this entire mission statement.

Another example is the relationship between African Americans and the ACLU. The ACLU was and is on the front lines when it came to civil rights and equality on race-based issues. The ACLU has championed issues such as voting rights and equity in criminal justice: issues which African Americans strongly support. However, the ACLU has also arguably led the charge on issues that are contrary to Scripture and basic values in the African American community. Categorically supporting the ACLU to some is not supporting Civil Rights, but rather is supporting intolerance and hate toward faith-based issues. There is a great necessity for African Americans to vocally and electorally evoke the line-item veto in terms of outlining support and disagreement for politics, policies, organizations, and candidates. Only in situations where individual issues are isolated, or when campaigns and candidates come down to single issues, is where the strong theological Conservatism in the African American community is expressed in voting participation.

While the lack of an electoral line-item veto may offer some context, probably the greatest explanation behind the dilemma facing African

American born-again Christians is the fundamental ideological and political issue regarding what is the proper role of government?

☛ **Point of Reflection:**

What is the proper role of government?

Role of Government:
Similar Philosophies... Expressed Differently

Conservatism, as the name suggests, argues in a favor of a limited government and protection of individual and states' rights. However, in the late '70s and early '80s during the expansion of the religious Right, Social Conservatives were now asking for an active central government in addressing a series of social issues. Social Conservatives made the case that abortion, gay and lesbian rights, prayers in schools, and later embryonic stem cell research were not just a matter of states' rights, privacy, or individual liberties, as argued with entitlement spending and other social programs. These were issues which the government should be very active in addressing. This brand of Conservatism distanced itself from the older Barry Goldwater and Nelson Rockefeller faction of Conservatism, which called for a limited government in both the bank account and the bedroom. Social Conservatives in essence made the argument that there was a moral law that should be included in all laws and that a reactive limited government that deferred to states' rights and individual liberties was not effective in properly addressing these issues. In essence, this is the same ideology on the role of government that has been the backbone of African American politics and history, but just expressed differently and targeted to additional issues.

African American history shows that the principles of individualism, hard work, self-responsibility, and little dependency on anyone other than God have been pillars at all stages of African American history. However, just as with Social Conservatism, there are a series of issues where many African Americans believe that a reactive limited government that defers to states' rights and individual liberties is not always effective in properly addressing certain challenges in our society. A strict states' rights advocate would argue, as did Barry Goldwater in the 1960s and Senator Rand Paul in 2011, that if a state, community, or individual did not want to integrate a school system, establish fair voting or employment laws, or had a discriminatory criminal justice system, then the federal government should stay out and let the states handle those issues.[67] Goldwater Republicans were against the Civil Rights Act of 1964 and more broadly the idea of Civil Rights as defined by many Americans at the time; Goldwater believed that a Civil Right is a right that is asserted and is therefore protected by some valid law. According to Goldwater, "Unless a right is incorporated into the law it is a Civil Right."[68] This philosophy believed that the scope of federal protection and enforcement should be limited to laws that were incorporated into government and not ideas that were socially or morally just but did not have a legal backing. African Americans depart from this strict states' rights/limited government philosophy and argue that there are basic civil and human rights, where a moral law should be infused into the discussion and government should be a bit more assertive in maintaining or establishing fundamental fairness. The shifts in American history from Slavery to Reconstruction, from Reconstruction to Jim Crow, from Jim Crow to Civil Rights and beyond ultimately came down to issues regarding the "role of government."

However, there have been influential thinkers among African Americans and Conservatives who make the case that there are other times where government can be a bit intrusive. Neither advocates a government that in any way compromises the freedom of speech or religion, and neither advocates any form of government that places any encumbrances to life, liberty, or the pursuit of happiness. But what we have in America among many African American and conservative Christian voters is a selectivity in determining when and on what issues the government should be passive and when the government should be active.

While both African Americans and Christian voters are not all-inclusive in their belief about the role of government, each appears to be inclusive about the role of government on issues involving fairness in opportunity, fairness in respecting morality, and protecting life; each revolves around the issue of justice, which is discussed in Question 2. The same motivation that drives an African American to view capital punishment with caution and thinks government should be more active in monitoring this issue is the same motivation that drives a Social Conservative to view abortion with caution and advocates for a more active government in monitoring and addressing this issue. It is the same ideological belief on life but just expressed differently. Unfortunately, differences in expression have widened the gap between African American voters at large and Christian voters at large and has exacerbated the dilemma for African Americans who are born-again Christians.

Question 2

ARE THERE STANDARDS THAT ALL CHRISTIANS AND/OR AFRICAN AMERICANS SHOULD ADHERE TO ON ELECTION DAY?

Faith-Based and Race-Based Reasoning

AT A VALUES Voter Summit on October 7, 2011, a pastor from Texas gave the following remarks during his introduction of a Republican presidential candidate:

> Do we want a candidate who is skilled in rhetoric or one who is skilled in leadership? Do we want a candidate who is a Conservative out of convenience or one who is a Conservative out of deep conviction? Do we want a candidate who is a good, moral person or do we want a candidate who is a born-again follower of the Lord Jesus Christ?[1]

Within hours of these comments being made, they became the lead story in nearly every major news outlet with the pastor being viewed negatively for these remarks. The comments were made in the context of Christian Conservative voters facing the reality of voting for a non-Christian in the upcoming election. The preponderance of criticism toward these remarks was based upon the pastor's use of faith-based reasoning. Faith-based reasoning is the practice of using faith as a tool to draw support from voters for a particular candidate or issue. Most major interest groups and organizations use some form of interest-based reasoning to attract political support. There is environmental reasoning, economic reasoning, educational reasoning, gender reasoning, disability reasoning, and race-based reasoning, as well as several other areas.

This brand of reasoning makes support or non-support of a particular candidate or issue as an overall indicator of support or lack of support for a greater cause. The challenge with these forms of reasoning is that they engage in generalizations, which often fail to capture the true nature of larger causes. This form of reasoning normally uses a moral and emotional pull to attract support for smaller issues. As a born-again Christian and African American, I have seen my fair share of both. However, when looking at the unique history of African Americans and the many components of Christianity that can be considered as absolute truth, discussion is necessary in assessing whether race-based or faith-based reasoning is necessary for either group. The large question is this:

☛ **Point of Reflection:**

Is there a biblical and/or racial line that all Christians and/or African Americans should adhere to on Election Day and in regards to politics in general?

Faith-Based Standards

All venues in society have sets of guiding principles that are in place to not only establish fairness but more importantly to give focus and direction. Society for the most part can accept the fact that rules and standards exist, except when it comes to the Bible. When the standards, ethics, and guidelines are introduced from a biblical perspective for issues, candidates, and politics, this causes great concern and anger that we must explore.

Absolutism: A concept found in all ideologies

Any discussion of *absolutes* on the surface will cause some to think of fanaticism or extremism; but in actuality, many theologies and belief systems have elements of absolutism. If an atheist is firm in his belief that there is no God, then he ultimately is absolute or dogmatic in his position of there being no God. If moral relativists or situational ethicists stand firm on their beliefs that values, morals, and ethics should be contingent on the situation and on each individual person's unique moral or ethical code, then they are definitive in their position that there are no moral or ethical definitives. If skeptics (regardless of degree) are those who take issue with objective truth, then to them their objective truth is that there is not any objective truth. So the idea of there being Christian absolutes is not out of sync with lines of thought in other ideological persuasions.

So, if a case can be made on the somewhat universal applicability of absolutism and standards in regards to faith and ethics, can the same argument be made purely from a racial perspective?

☞ **Point of Reflection:**

Are there African American dogmas or political standards?

From the classic W.E.B. Du Bois and Booker T. Washington disagreements in methods of seeking political and economic empowerment to Malcolm and Martin's disagreements on methods of fighting discrimination to the present day *massive* dissention among African Americans in terms of critiquing President Obama's policy record, the challenge has existed for years in the development or necessity of there being race-based political standards or rules of engagement.

The task of finding absolutes or dogmas from exclusively an African American perspective is a bit challenging because there is no divinely inspired book, moral document, or set of guiding principles that determines what is and isn't Black. Many individuals and organizations have attempted to establish African American standards or values in politics. But what has been the consistent stumbling block is when other variables are added to race such as faith, generations (age), geography, and economics. When these factors enter the picture, it becomes very difficult to find a very large set of issues or values that all Blacks could or more importantly should be morally bound to support.

"Just because it *is* does not mean it *ought to be*."

In August of 2007 the NAACP did a report entitled, *Public Opinion in Black and White: The More Things Change, the More They Stay the Same.* This report analyzed the differences in perspectives between Whites and Blacks on a series of issues. The report revealed that there are still some major divisions that exist between the races on a number of issues.[2] The report also indirectly revealed that there were some issues that caused a significant divide internally among Blacks. For example, nearly 40 percent of Black men said that they would "definitely" or "likely" support a candidate who supports the death penalty; this percentage was 8 percentage points higher than Black women, which suggests this is not a point of internal harmony among Blacks at large or even among Black men.[3] Nearly 60 percent of Blacks said that they would support a candidate who was for school vouchers, leaving 40 percent who did not take this same position, again suggesting that there are major differences within the Black community on a series of issues.[4] If we look at other studies on issues of healthcare or immigration, we will find the same trend, which is that not all African Americans have the same goals in mind, or if similar goals are shared, oftentimes the debate comes on how the goal should be attained. In terms of voting trends among African Americans we know what "is," but the trouble comes in determining what "ought to be." The point is there are very few areas where we can say that all African Americans are ethically or morally bound to support, so divisions on certain issue cannot be considered a problem if there is no ethical guide that determines what voting trends "ought to be."

In Question 1 we discussed indifferent and definitive issues solely from a biblical perspective, and we discovered that there is a much larger base of indifferent issues than definitive issues. This trend is also in place when looking at issues from a solely African American perspective. The trouble comes when we insert dogmatism from our own personal perspectives that are purely based upon our experiences.

This is what President Obama was referring to during his speech on race during the 2008 campaign, when he discussed the comments that were being made by Dr. Jeremiah Wright. President Obama alluded to the fact that Dr. Wright came from a time period where issues of segregation and discrimination were far more overt than in his personal experience. These differences in experience were the cause of stronger attitudes of mistrust toward the government and those of other races by some in Dr. Wright's generation. Again this does not validate the comments made by Dr. Wright, but it further illustrates that one's position on race-related issues is not only influenced by race but also by generational, cultural, and geographical experience.

Barack Obama's first book, *Dreams from My Father*, was in many respects his quest to discover his own racial identity. As a young man with an African father and a Caucasian mother, being raised in Indonesia and later Hawaii, he was on a quest to discover what being Black was. He was not raised in an inner-city metropolitan area, nor was he raised in the poverty-stricken South. However, are we to suggest that he is not authentically Black because his life experience does not reflect that of other minorities? Unfortunately, what will find is that experiential socialization or the "what is" will constantly affect one's views on race or the "what ought to be."

QUESTION 2: Are There Standards That All Christians and/or
African Americans Should Adhere To on Election Day?

31

The Search for Black Authenticity

In 1993 with the back drop of the highly controversial Clarence Thomas Supreme Court confirmation hearings and riots that occurred in Los Angeles as a result of the Rodney King trial, Dr. Cornel West wrote his bestselling book, *Race Matters*. In the book he argued against what he called racial authenticity. Dr. West points out that one of the things that led to Thomas's confirmation was his appeal to racial authenticity, based upon his use of his experiences growing up in the South, which included a history of poverty and racism. It was this appeal to race, according to Dr. West, that caused many African American leaders from different ideological and political backgrounds to not focus on Thomas's credentials and ideological record and to focus on his appeal to race.[5] Dr. West used his confirmation hearings as an example to argue that in America we should stay away from racial reasoning or attempting to define what is or isn't authentically Black. In turn we should take a more prophetic perspective which is rooted in moral reasoning. This style of reasoning focuses more on issues of ethics and character than skin color when making decisions about candidates and politics. Dr. West calls this level of reasoning a "Mature Black Identity," which values variances and democracy in Black thought and identity.[6] Dr. West goes as far as to contend that racial reasoning discourages moral reasoning on the grounds that racial reasoning clouds many of the political, economic, and ethnic factors that go into decision making.[7] Dr. West points out that one's personal experience should not either validate, invalidate, lessen, or improve one's level of Black authenticity.[8]

Despite Dr. West's overarching appeal to avoid a definition or litmus test of Black authenticity, he offers a very brief description of what he believes being Black must constitute. According to Dr. West, "Being Black means being minimally subject to White supremacist abuse and being part of a rich culture and community that has struggled against such abuse. All people with Black skin and African phenotype are subject to potential White supremacist abuse."[9] While Dr. West claims that any definition or criteria above the ones that he has highlighted is purely subjective,[10] one has to wonder is there any subjectivity in his definition? Is the conception of being subject to White supremacy a generational construct? That is not to say that racism is not alive in our society and that acts of supremacy are not still possible; but from a global perspective in today's culture, is there the possibility of Black people at large being

subject to White supremacy? Is there enough Black economic and political capital as well as internal organization to fend off a threat of White
supremacy? Does there need to be greater organization and unity among
African Americans in regards to the economic and fiscal empowerment?
I would presume that one's response to these questions would be purely
ideological and less empirical. The slippery slope of Black authenticity is
that while it attempts to validate Blackness, at the same time it indirectly
invalidates other forms of Blackness. Therefore, am I more Black because
I grew up in inner city Philadelphia than a Black person who grew up
in Montana? Am I more Black because I went to a HBCU than a person
who did not? Is a person who grew up living in the projects on welfare
more Black than a person who grew up in an upper middle class home?
Were the Evans (*Good Times*) more Black then the Huxtables (the *Cosby
Show*)? Who is more Black? Those who have light skin or those who
have dark skin? These stigmas and stereotypes are weeds that we have
allowed to grow in the garden of the African American culture, and the
only weed killer that can maintain the beauty and harmony of African
Americans is faith. Here is where I believe again that it is difficult to iso-
late any discussion or definition of race from faith.

Faith and Race Forever Connected (Joined at the Hip)

Dr. West's contention that being Black involves the potential of being
subject to White supremacist abuse was an argument that laid the foundation for another one of his arguments about the greatest issue facing
African Americans. He contends that the biggest issue facing Black
America is not "structural constraints" which are a decrease in effective
governmental systems and programs, as the Liberals contend. Nor is it
an increase in lascivious behavior and unethical practices on public and
personal levels, as the Conservatives would contend. Rather, the greatest
threat is a pervasive feeling of nihilism. Dr West defines nihilism as "a
philosophical doctrine that there are no rational grounds for legitimate
standards or authority; it is, far more, the lived experience of coping
with a life of horrifying meaningless, hopelessness, and (most important)
lovessness."[11] Dr West attributes the spread of nihilism to the shattering
of Black institutions, neighborhoods, schools, churches, and families,[12]
by the hands of the disproportionate amounts of capital, power, and
resources in the corporate market place.[13] Dr. West contends that the
only tools that can control nihilism are the tools of love and care. Here

QUESTION 2: Are There Standards That All Christians and/or
African Americans Should Adhere To on Election Day?

33

is where I will take it a step further. Love is rooted in a faith, a faith that is centered on God because "God is love" (1 John 4:8). So it is difficult to have a discussion on issues of race without looking at the solution of faith. While these factors may indeed exist, the tools of dismantling them must be dealt with, by, and through faith. But there is one standard that I suggest which finds its roots in faith and the history of our country, that all Americans have some degree of affinity for, and that may provide a political standard for all African Americans and all Christians.

Justice: A Biblical and Constitutional Standard

The fight and frustration that has almost defined African Americans politics and culture in several forms has almost exclusively rested with equality and fairness, which can be summed up by the standard or principle of justice. Justice is both a biblical and constitutional right guaranteed to all people. The standard of justice says that all people in the eyes of God and in the eyes of government have the right to be treated equally and fairly under the law. If there is no law or standard that guides what is right, then the standard of justice can never exist.

The year 2012 marks the twenty-year anniversary of the Rodney King beatings, which brought up a series of discussion in America about that very controversial moment in America's history; it ultimately came down to issues regarding race relations and justice. There was anger and frustration in America when the beating of motorist Rodney King was revealed; however, anger quickly turned into rage when those who beat him were found not guilty in a questionable criminal trial. That decision and the handling of the trial were seen as a threat to justice. In 2012 there was anger and hurt when the teenager Trayvon Martin was shot and killed; anger again turned into massive frustration when his known killer was not arrested until there was massive civil unrest. Again, this was a threat to justice. In the above scenarios, as well as several others, the greatest frustration was not with the beatings or the killing, but more so with the absence of justice or fundamental fairness in the aftermath of each tragic event. We can also look at the rising prison population in America overall, in comparison to other nations; as well as the disproportionate number of African American males that are incarcerated, with both issues bringing up serious concerns with criminal *justice*.[14]

In biblical thought, God's grace justifies men from their evil deeds, and they are now seen as righteous in God's eyes. The United States'

Declaration of Independence reinforces this idea when it states in its second sentence:

> We hold these truths to be self-evident, that all men are created equal, that they are endowed by their Creator with certain unalienable rights, that among these are life, liberty and the pursuit of happiness.

Our country's founding documents discuss the idea of God giving man certain unalienable rights, meaning that these rights cannot be taken away. The first line of the Preamble to the Constitution reiterates this biblical concept by stating, "We the People of the United States, in Order to form a more perfect Union, establish *Justice*" (emphasis added). Here we have a standard that the church and state both recognize; that all people and all situations are to be handled equitably under the law.

The legal and theological stumbling block that many have with the standard of justice is that it not only involves recompense for good deeds but it also involves recompense for violations of the law or *injustice*. It is easy to celebrate a loving God and a just government that sees no wrong in any actions; but whenever there is a government or God that recompenses negative actions, some may rethink how they feel about either. God, in His infinite wisdom, will judge the hearts and minds of men, and we leave that exclusively to Him. The government, under its legal domain, judges the deeds and actions of men. The standard of justice holds the government accountable that it is living up to its founding principles, with citizens being treated equally under the law. So what we have in justice is a legal and spiritual standard that is rooted in faith and affects all races.

Any dogmatism about race must be coupled with faith; and it is through these bifocals that we stare into some of the issues facing our generation.

SECTION II
THE DEAL BREAKERS

Question 3

POVERTY:
WHOSE RESPONSIBILITY IS IT;
CHURCH, GOVERNMENT, OR INDIVIDUAL?

Economics in America

RECENTLY I WAS in a supermarket shopping during the evening hours; as I was placing my groceries on the conveyer belt, I noticed that many of the workers in the store started pointing and zealously trying to get the attention of the police officer on duty. As I looked to the door, I noticed a man running out of the store; at the same time one of the workers in the market was standing by the door holding several packages of meat, gravy, and other items of food that were retrieved out of the man's jacket as he was trying to leave the store. The police officers on duty ran out of the store chasing the man. As they apprehended him and brought him back into the store, I heard him yelling, "I am hungry!" This unfortunate, heartbreaking, yet common scenario is but one story of many about poverty; a legitimate, widespread and serious issue in our society. Even more significant than that: the Bible has much to say about this topic.

One could take a legalistic approach to the man in the supermarket and only see that he has broken one of the Ten Commandments; however when I delve into the issue that this man had to steal just to eat, it opens the door for a wide discussion. Was this man employed? Was this man unemployed? Was he a good steward of his money? Did he make the decision not to find a job? Was he lazy? Was his hunger due to a bad economy?

Some in America will go to foreign nations and feed the hungry, which I believe Christians are commissioned to do, while neglecting the hungry here in America. Arguably, the reason why some are more compassionate toward the poor abroad is because they feel that the poor in foreign countries are impoverished based on no fault of their own, while those in America are living in poverty based upon bad decisions and laziness. The Bible does have some very clear, direct, and harsh language when it comes to working and to those who make the decision not to work. At the same time the Bible does not offer any preconditions for ministering (or serving) to the poor. Jesus told a group of His disciples,

> For I was hungered, and ye gave me meat: I was thirsty and ye gave me drink: I was a stranger and ye took me in: Naked, and ye clothed me: I was sick and ye visited me: I was in prison and ye came unto me....In as much as ye have done unto one of the least of these my brethren, ye have done unto me.[1]

Notice Jesus did not make any mention as to the cause of their hunger and nakedness. His primary concern was that the needs of this group were being addressed. While these along with many others passages clearly indicate that God is concerned with the needs of the poor and gives the charge to meet the needs of the poor and impoverished, there are two underlying questions that always come up when attempting to deal with issues of poverty. The first question is how should poverty be addressed? And the second question is whose responsibility is it: should the church, the government, or the impoverished have primary responsibility for addressing this issue?

What appears to be happening is the church gets frustrated at the government for not doing more, the government creates programs that try to get the church more involved, while the impoverished appear to be waiting on the church and the government to step up to the plate. As a result of this apparent passing of the buck, the church, government, and impoverished are failing to take ownership of this issue.

There also is another question that must be answered when dealing with poverty that precedes issues of accountability and methodology: What is the ultimate goal?

☛ **Point of Reflection:**

Poverty, end it or control it?

- "The poor you will always have with you."[2]

- "There will always be poor people in the land. Therefore
  I command you to be openhanded toward your brothers
  and toward the poor and needy in your land."[3]

Countless books, articles, seminars, and interest groups have been formed to tackle the nearly infinite issues surrounding poverty, but any effective study on this issue must begin with the question: Can poverty be abolished in America or can it only be controlled?

First, from a biblical perspective, above we find the words of Jesus that indicate that the poor will always be with us; this is somewhat of an affirmation of the words of God in the old covenant as given through Moses in the second quote. This does not in any way take away the urgency or necessity of addressing poverty on a consistent basis; but rather it starts the discussion off with the understanding that regardless of any effort, missions work, or governmental programs, this cancer will always remain to a certain extent. This is a tough pill to swallow for any minister, activist, or ordinary citizen who has a concern for those that are without; but what this biblical perspective tells us is that the focus must be on decreasing and curtailing the number of those who are living in poverty.

From an economic perspective, poverty will always exist in a society whose economy allows choice, options, and competition. The backbone of capitalism is choice, as opposed to suppression, oppression, and forced behavior as defined by the economic and governmental alternatives. While I am not suggesting that one economic perspective carries greater biblical authority than another, the main differences in economic philosophies, as we will delve into in greater detail in this chapter, is the issue of choice and individual decision making. Choice in and of itself is not the cause of poverty, but it does place massive responsibility on the decision maker. Even when systems and programs are in place to assist those who have not had the full capability or resources to make decisions about their economic futures, these systems have not rescued people from the bands of poverty but rather have provided comfort and minimum resources while they are still in poverty; this is what we will see in the many attempts by government to resolve poverty.

From a cultural perspective, we have discovered in the previous chapter that any assumptions or ideas of cultural authenticity or ethical homogeny will always be rooted in a bias. While our study focused on African Americans, the concept can apply to the other populous cultures in America as well. If everyone in the culture does not have the same philosophical, societal, or theological perspective, then it logically follows that there will be varying economic perspectives. Put simply, some will work and some won't. These varying perspectives will mean that some will fall into the traps of poverty, while others will not.

However, facts indicate that African Americans are disproportionately impoverished as compared to other ethnicities. In addition, a recent study made a case that African Americans have become the face of the alleged undeserving poor in America.

The Racialization of Poverty: The Deserving and Undeserving Poor

A recent study made the case that there has been a racialization of poverty, with African Americans becoming the face of poverty, laziness, government waste, and what some would consider the undeserving poor, which has led to an increase in negative attitudes about programs that support the impoverished.[4]

The study examined coverage of issues related to poverty in a series of major national news magazines over a forty-year period and found the volume and percentage of images of African Americans were strongly disproportionate to the percentage of African Americans that were actually in poverty. Overall for much of the forty-year period, there was an increase in stories on poverty although poverty rates were decreasing. During this time African Americans accounted for over 50 percent of poor people pictured in news stories, despite the fact that African Americans were actually only 29.3 percent of the poor during this time.[5] This trend reached its apex in 1967 with Blacks being seen in 72 percent of the images related to poverty while the number of African Americans actually in poverty remained stable.[6] It is a safe assumption that these images indeed have shaped public perception of African Americans for many years in relation to poverty.[7]

This study also found that besides an increase in images of African Americans in stories related to poverty, there were also a disproportionate number of images of African Americans in stories that were very critical of the impoverished and viewed them as being lazy and undeserving. In the reverse, stories that were more sympathetic toward the impoverished, which ran normally around times of national economic crises such as in the late '70s and early '80s, saw fewer images of African

Americans in them.[8] The discrepancies in tone and image have perpetuated beliefs in America that African Americans are the essence of the poor in America and that African Americans are also the embodiment of the undeserving poor in America.

According to recent census data, there are 43.6 million people in America that are living in poverty.[9] Of that amount 9.94 million are African Americans, which represents roughly 23 percent of the impoverished, meaning that over 70 percent of the impoverished in America are not African Americans.[10] While there is indeed a gross disparity of African Americans living in poverty, which can be seen in the fact that roughly 12 percent of the population is African American, yet African Americans represent 23 percent of the impoverished,[11] however, overall statistics tell us that poverty is an American problem.

So with an understanding that poverty will always exist and that it negatively impacts all Americans, with a disproportionately high number of African Americans living in poverty, the goal then focuses on containing and decreasing the numbers that are living in poverty and working to cease poverty from spreading from one generation to the next. Now we can turn our attention to establishing accountability and effective methods for addressing poverty—looking at the church, government, and the individual responsibility for addressing poverty.

☛ **Point of Reflection:**

Is poverty the church's responsibility?

Of each of the issues that we will address in the latter half of this book, poverty, and more broadly economics, is the most complicated in terms of delineating a clear line of thought on spending.

The main argument in favor of the church having primary accountability and ownership for addressing poverty is the idea that when Jesus spoke about feeding the hungry, clothing the naked, and preaching to gospel to the poor, He was talking to His disciples and therefore to the church. If His communication was to the church, then this is where ownership for the issue must rest. Throughout Jesus' ministry on earth, He consistently trained, taught, and gave direction to His disciples; while there was an expectation for government to do what was right, Jesus became frustrated when His followers did not do His will. From a biblical perspective, addressing poverty would appear to be an issue where the church must take direct ownership. There have been many different approaches by the church to deal with addressing poverty. Let's start with one of the relatively newer methods of addressing poverty that has caused some controversy and great debate— teaching on biblical prosperity.

☛ **Point of Reflection:**

Is biblical prosperity an answer to poverty?

Recently I was talking to a focus group and asked them what their greatest concern was in the church. They stated that they were concerned that too many preachers were corrupting the gospel by placing an undue amount of attention on issues surrounding health and wealth. Later in the conversation, I asked the same group which issues would primarily control their voting decisions on Election Day; the primary response from the group was the economy and healthcare. I stated to them that those issues sound a lot like health and wealth to me. What this suggests is that issues of economics, fiscal responsibility, and health are indeed both significant in the church and in politics. Disagreements are formed when the discussion goes to how these issues are addressed and who will address them.

Prosperity Theology vs. Social Justice Theology: What Is Good News to the Poor?

There have been two major theologies that have become the backbone of the church's response to poverty. The first is the theology of the Social Gospel, as described in Question 2, and the other is the more recent doctrine or covenant of prosperity. The doctrine of biblical prosperity is similar to the Social Gospel in that it illustrates God's concern for the poor and less affluent. However, when it comes to interpreting Scripture, the prosperity doctrine differs from the Social Gospel on its worldview of economics, God's position on wealth, major ideological frameworks, and how to best address poverty. In some respects the distinctions between the two can be seen in how they interpret Jesus' message in the first line of His first sermon in Luke 4:18:

> The Spirit of the Lord is upon me because he has anointed me to preach the gospel to the poor.

For the most part there is no disagreement that Jesus has a legitimate concern for the poor and views poverty as one of His top priorities. The question comes down to how the needs of this group are addressed or what constitutes preaching the gospel (good news) to the poor? An advocate of the Social Gospel interprets this message primarily as compassion, justice, and love for the poor while they remain in poverty, while the prosperity doctrine primarily interprets this message as a focus on teaching the poor that there is a way out of poverty, with God not placing limits on how far out one can go.

Biblical Prosperity and Poverty

The message of biblical prosperity is one of the most polarizing issues in modern Christendom. Most people either fall into one of two camps on this issue; they either openly welcome it as a component of salvation that has been neglected for many years or they view it as being heretical, fraudulent, and cancerous to the Christian message.

Regardless of one's theological persuasion, most students of Scripture will agree that the Bible has a lot to say about the subject of economics, finances, and wealth. More specifically, Jesus spoke more on these subjects than He did about prayer, sin, or salvation. Some will contend that His frequent discussions on economics were done so metaphorically or to illustrate other spiritual truths. Regardless of whether it was done metaphorically or for the purpose of directly teaching on the subject of economics, we know for certain that in the vast majority of Jesus' recorded teachings, He referenced economics.

According to the prosperity gospel teaching, being financially prosperous in and of itself can have nothing to do with God. An atheist who exercises good financial decision-making can become fiscally prosperous. So then, biblical prosperity encompasses more than just fiscal prosperity. In other words, money is not the only component of biblical prosperity, but it is *a* component.

The message of prosperity finds its origins, like most of Christian theology, in the Old Testament. When the children of Israel were leaving Egyptian captivity and were on their way to the Promised Land, God made a covenant with them, recorded in Deuteronomy 28, indicating that if they remained obedient and faithful to God, which involves living an ethically sound and morally righteous life[12] and practicing economic stewardship (wise financial decisions), then God would bless them and prosper them in all areas of their lives. Biblical prosperity cannot be achieved exclusively by living an ethically sound lifestyle or exclusively by making wise financial decisions, but rather a combination of the two.

Jesus' ministry continued on the teachings of this covenant. In one instance, Jesus teaches that if we place God's work ahead of our own, blessings will come to the believer. Then, in chapter 3 of the Book of Galatians, the apostle Paul draws a bridge between the Old Testament covenant promise and all New Testament believers by illustrating that Christ's sacrifice entitles New Testament believers to share in the Old Testament covenant promises or blessings.

There are several other passages in the Bible that continue on this same vein. The two most quoted scriptures that affirm this position are 3 John 2 from the New Testament and Deuteronomy 8:18 from the Old Testament.

> Beloved, I wish above all things that thou mayest prosper and be in health, even as thy soul prospereth.
>
> —3 JOHN 2

> But Thou shalt remember the Lord thy God: for it is he that giveth thee power to get wealth, the he may establish his covenant.
>
> —DEUTERONOMY 8:18

The first passage indicates that biblical prosperity encompasses mental, physical, emotional, and fiscal prosperity as a biblical covenant promise that is rooted in God's love for all believers. The second passage indicates God will give His people strategies and ideas to accumulate wealth and to achieve God's mission. God blesses or prospers the church to be in a position to minister to the world.

This theology began to gain prominence in the late '60s and early '70s. Ironically, this was also when Lyndon Johnson began his war on poverty and poverty rates in America were at some of their highest points. This theology really gained a wide following in the African American community. Of late, some of the main proponents of the prosperity message are African American preachers. Many prominent African American preachers embrace some if not all of the prosperity doctrine. This theology challenged the notion of the more traditional view that poverty was a symbol of holiness, or that God was indifferent toward economic success. The traditional view on God and money put forth the idea that through faith in Christ salvation is guaranteed, eternal life is guaranteed, and peace is guaranteed, but economic stability is left up to chance. Financial security was either not important or was exclusively a matter of divine providence.

The biggest questions that arose to challenge the prosperity message was about Jesus' personal economic position and His alleged negative disposition toward economic affluence or wealth.

☞ Point of Reflection:

Was Jesus poor and does He hate the rich?

The biggest challenge that has been presented to the covenant of prosperity is the belief that Jesus was poor and that He was categorically against any and all forms of economic affluence and prosperity. In one occasion Jesus was confronted by a rich young ruler, who Jesus gave the opportunity to be one of His disciples. Jesus told him, "Sell [all] that thou hast, and give to the poor, and thou shalt have treasure in heaven: and come and follow me" (Matt. 19:21). When the rich man struggled with giving away his goods, Jesus condemned him for his greed (v. 23). In another place during Jesus' Sermon on the Mount, He began His teaching on ethics, commonly referred to as the Beatitudes, with the phrase, "Blessed are the poor in spirit, for theirs is the kingdom of heaven" (Matt. 5:3).

For many years the classic interpretation of Jesus' economic position was that He lived a humble life in poverty and this was the example that Christians should follow. This was in many respects the backbone of Rauschenbusch's Social Gospel. Rauschenbusch's contention that being poor was equitable with being godly and meek clearly places God on the side of the poor and against any and all forms of economic stability or success.[13] This belief advocated that Jesus was primarily and exclusively concerned about the poor and that He saw material possessions, wealth, and the wealthy as being evil. As a result, for many years churches completely stayed away from any major discussions on money, finances, or wealth. They based their beliefs upon two primary passages:

> For the love of money is the root of all evil: which while some coveted after, they have erred from the faith, and pierced themselves through with many sorrows.
>
> —1 Timothy 6:10

> No servant can serve two masters: for either he will hate the one, and love the other; or else he will hold to the one, and despise the other. Ye cannot serve God and mammon [money].
>
> —Luke 16:13

The Prosperity Theology challenges this interpretation and argues that these passages were not referring to God categorically being against the rich, but rather God being against those that served, coveted, or loved money. In this view, money in and of itself is not evil, but rather the controlling desire by some to obtain money was evil. The Prosperity Theology argues that Jesus' position on economics is not against wealth or affluence.

☛ **Point of Reflection:**

Was Jesus rich and did He fight against poverty?

There are also a series of valuable arguments that suggest that Jesus did not live a life of poverty. These arguments include the fact that Jesus was born in a stall because there was no room in the inn, not because his parents lacked the resources to place Him in an inn. The Bible records that when Jesus was born, He was presented with frankincense, myrrh, and gold—gifts for a king. During His adult years, the disciples traveled with Him on a full-time basis, meaning that Jesus had twelve full-time followers or employees, one of whom was Judas, who was Jesus' treasurer, the person who gave to the poor. There were not only funds to sustain the twelve men who also had to support their families, but there were also funds to give to the poor. In addition, the men who Jesus chose as His disciples were businessmen. Both James and John were entrepreneurs in their father's fishing business, Simon and Andrew also had their own fishing business, and Matthew was a tax collector. This illustrates that some of Jesus' disciples were men who had a strong economic background. So Jesus surrounded Himself with men who were versed in economics, and the majority of His teachings were about economics to groups of people who were impoverished.

Even a commonly quoted scripture by the apostle Paul which is used to validate Jesus' poverty hints at the idea the Jesus was not impoverished; the apostle Paul states, "He became poor" (2 Cor. 8:9). This, according to Prosperity Theology, gives the connotation that He chose poverty and illustrates that He had wealth but made the decision to become or identify with the impoverished. This view holds that Jesus was not disenchanted with wealth but was more so disenchanted with haughty attitudes and arrogance by some who were wealthy, such as in the case of the rich man in his encounter with Lazarus.

In addition, the Bible records that Abraham was "very rich," Solomon had great wealth and used it to build God a temple, and King Josiah used his wealth to honor God with one of the greatest Passover celebrations in the history of the feast. So this theology teaches that wealth in the hands of those with godly intentions is a vehicle in preaching good news to the poor.

On a broader level, whether Jesus was impoverished or not, we see Him consistently ministering to the poor, destitute, and less affluent. Some have argued that God has determined where everyone's economic position in life will be and that everybody is not called or destined to be fiscally prosperous.

☛ **Points of Reflection:**

Is economic stability or prosperity predestined?

Are some predestined to be poor, while others are predestined to be rich, and others are predestined to be middle class?

Here is the challenge of discussion on biblical economics: if God has predestined some to be poor, then why should there be any discussion on helping the impoverished to rise above their current economic condition? Should churches and community action organizations fight for jobs for the poor? Or should they fight for jobs that only will allow the impoverished to meet their minimum needs or just remain in the middle class? Is the middle class God's ideal economic stratum?

Long-Term and Short-Term Methods from the Church in Addressing Poverty

So the Social Gospel and prosperity doctrine represent the two main approaches from the church in addressing poverty. Prosperity Theology sees the work of the church as providing teaching and training for poor people to lead them out of their predicament through self-sufficiency. The Social Gospel sees the work of the church as providing resources and sustenance to the poor and challenging the government to do more in terms of providing resources for poor people. So the church's primary responses to poverty have been either primarily advocating self-sufficiency or increased government intervention.

Is Poverty the Government's Responsibility?

We the People of the United States, in Order to form a more perfect Union, establish Justice, insure domestic Tranquility, provide for the common defence, promote the general Welfare, and secure the

Blessings of Liberty to ourselves and our Posterity, do ordain and establish this Constitution for the United States of America.
—PREAMBLE OF THE UNITED STATES CONSTITUTION

The belief of governmental accountability for poverty is rooted in the ideals of America's founding fathers as expressed in the Preamble of the United States Constitution. The ideals of justice, tranquility, welfare, and liberty served as the pillars that supported America, with an understanding that government would have some responsibility in ensuring that these pillars were in place for all citizens. Since the inception of the country, there has always been and there probably always will be differences of opinion in the economic area. One of the best examples we find of economic differences in America overall was the competing attitudes in the years following the Civil War about the role of the federal government during the period of Reconstruction.

The Freedmen's Bureau: A "Case-Study" of Competing Economic Ideologies

In the years immediately following the Civil War, America went through a series of changes. The Emancipation Proclamation freed many slaves. However, these former slaves did not have any property, finances, or training to sustain themselves. In order to address these needs, President Lincoln created the Bureau of Refugees, Freedmen, and Abandoned Lands in March of 1865, frequently referred to as the Freedmen's Bureau. The purpose of this organization was to successfully transition former slaves from a life of slavery into a life of freedom via programs that were targeted toward providing assistance to the former slaves in labor, land, and education.

Regarding labor, the Freedmen's Bureau helped to facilitate a system of fair labor practices in the South which included conducting negotiations between the former slaves and plantation owners.[14] In regards to land, the bill that created the Freedmen's Bureau in March of 1865 also mandated that the federal government provide not more than forty acres of land to freed slaves to establish themselves and their families.[15] In regards to education, the Bureau established and managed schools which taught many of the former slaves how to read and write.[16] Probably the greatest legacy of the educational initiative of the Freedmen's Bureau was the establishment of many Historically Black Colleges and Universities via partnership with the American Missionary Association.[17]

Within a month after the founding of the Freedmen's Bureau, President Lincoln was assassinated and a new Administration came to power that had a completely different perspective on the extent of government intervention during Reconstruction. For the years that followed, there was massive division and conflict between the new Administration under President Andrew Johnson and Congress on this very issue.

On the one hand, there were many in the country that carried discriminatory and racist attitudes toward many of the former slaves, which was the basis for their overall opposition to the Freedmen's Bureau and government's involvement in assisting the former slaves. However, there were also massive economic ideological differences that surfaced during this time. These differences led to the ultimate demise of the Bureau and the relatively short life span of Reconstruction in the South.

President Johnson represented a political ideology that believed that the government should not take an aggressive role in interfering in state affairs or in creating programs that allegedly built "dependency on the government."[18] President Johnson was also an outspoken segregationist who did not share Lincoln's vision for Reconstruction. This belief was also coupled with the idea that the federal government should take a very limited role in ensuring that former Confederate States were adhering to and respecting the laws and rights of the freed slaves in the years immediately following the Civil War. This is the main position that Johnson and others along his same ideology would use in their attack on Reconstruction and on the creation of government programs to assist the destitute and impoverished.[19]

During the years following the Civil War, it was President Johnson, along with many Southern Democrats, who championed states' rights and limited government versus a faction known as the "Radical Republicans" who supported massive government intervention in guaranteeing equality and justice for the newly freed African Americans. Ultimately, the Southern Democrats were successful in their bid to minimize government intervention in ensuring economic justice and basic civil and human rights to the newly freed slaves. As a result, Reconstruction ended after only thirteen years, and the south entered into the turbulent Jim Crow era. As previously stated, the shift in America from slavery to Reconstruction, from Reconstruction to Jim Crow, from Jim Crow to the Civil Rights Movement ultimately came down to the degree of government intervention.

There have been many questions and issues that surrounded this time in American history that are in many ways the same questions that resound to this very day in regards to economic policy and the role of the government in addressing poverty. The primary question is: To what extinct should the government play a role in the economy and addressing poverty? In addition, how much is too much?

Poverty from the Left: Is Government the Answer?

Throughout African American history, many of the major strides that were accomplished were as a result of government taking some kind of action. However, it must be noted that government's actions were influenced by the persistence of those on the outside or *individuals* fighting for what they believed was right. If government failed to take action, then the marches, protests, demonstrations, and boycotts would have been fruitless. The right to vote, freedom from slavery, integration, the establishment of the vast majority of Historically Black Colleges and Universities all were direct products of government intervention. Even more broadly, the right for women to vote, protection from enemies both foreign and domestic, the right to bear arms, and the right to religious freedom all have come about via government action and protection. Therefore, the idea of looking to the federal government for redress has some universal applicability that transcends all races, income stratums, and the vast majority of all ideologies.

Present day Liberalism sees government as the *primary and at times exclusive* answer to many of the challenges facing the culture. Naturally, when it comes to poverty, a Liberal advocates for a more aggressive and progressive government.

Modern Liberalism

In many ways, present day Liberalism is strongly influenced by the principles expressed by British economist John Maynard Keynes. Keynes believed that during times of economic instability and massive unemployment (which arguably is perpetual), that it was right for the government to continue spending, run up deficits, invest in public works programs such as infrastructures, and to create programs to increase and spur aggregate demand.[20] Aggregate demand according to Keynes is the belief that "demand would create supply."[21] Keynes argued that consumption and spending would spur supply and thus raise income and help stabilize the economy during troubled times. Keynes idea was for the government to play a major role in rehabilitating the economy through massive spending.

Keynes was in many respects and informal advisor to President Franklin Delano Roosevelt and in some ways his ideas were an inspiration for President Roosevelt's New Deal policies which were rooted in massive government intervention to help spur the economy in the years following the depression.[22] During the Roosevelt Administration, America saw the expansion of government spending and the seeds were planted for what has become the welfare state in America. This is the state of addressing poverty through direct government intervention, with many residents in a country getting direct support in the form of cash, goods, and services from the government.

The Social Security Act of 1935 in many respects was the starting point for massive government intervention on the federal level or welfare spending in America. The highlights of this Act was the establishment of federally funded old age benefits (commonly referred to as Retirement Benefits or Social Security), Aid to Families with Dependent Children (AFDC), and federal assistance to States for unemployment compensation. Progressively since this act was signed, via both Democrat and Republican Presidents, government assistance and direct intervention has expanded, and America has arguably entered into a state of being where most of its citizens depend on government intervention. According to a *Wall Short Journal* article, in the first quarter of 2011 nearly 50 percent of the population received some form of government benefit.[23]

☞ **Point of Reflection:**

　Is America a welfare state?

Rich, Middle Class, and Poor
All Benefit from Welfare in America

The term *welfare* has become synonymous with the General Assistance program (a state-sponsored program that offers small cash payments to single adults) or the Temporary Assistance to Needy Families program (TANF), formerly AFDC, which is a federal government program that offers cash payments to single parents who have children. These along with other means-tested programs such as Food Stamps and low-income housing, which target the poor, have become synonymous with representing welfare in America. But the reality is welfare or government (social) spending is very large and encompasses programs that support the rich, middle class, and poor. The argument can be made that each income stratum in America benefits from social spending. Government welfare programs include social insurance programs, means-tested programs, and educational programs.

Social insurance programs

Social insurance programs are government programs that target a specific population such as seniors, the disabled, unemployed, etc., where the recipients pay a premium into the program (normally through taxes) and receive a benefit based upon their contributions. Normally social programs are mandatory for all citizens, with the government bearing the responsibility for the risk. In social insurance programs, premiums are virtually the same for all recipients, which is much different than the private sector and significantly increasing the risk. The payout or government benefit is guaranteed (backed by the federal government), with government having the ability to alter benefits and payment structure; and generally the benefits are equitable for all recipients. In America, Social Security fits many of the above criteria, with many of the governmental changes to the program arguably benefiting the poor.[24]

In America, Social Security is a pay-as-you-go system, meaning receipts from the taxes of current workers provide benefits for current retirees, as opposed to each person's actual tax contributions going into their own individual account. These factors arguably make programs such as Social Security and Medicare considered as part of welfare programs in America.

Means-tested programs

These are programs that primarily target the poor and are based upon meeting certain income and resource requirements. Funding for these programs comes directly from general treasury dollars.

Education

These are programs where the federal government (with state government also playing a large part) subsidizing free education, which is mandatory for all children from kindergarten through twelfth grade. The government also provides grants, scholarships, and subsidized loans for postsecondary education.

Social insurance spending has the largest percentage of welfare (social spending) in America, with some demographics such as senior citizens, veterans, and the disabled receiving two or even all three forms of government welfare spending.[25] For example, in 2011 the United States federal budget was roughly $3.6 trillion dollars.[26] Of the two most discussed means-tested programs, Supplemental Nutritional Assistance Program (formerly Food Stamps) accounted for roughly 2 percent of the federal budget[27] and Temporary Assistance to Needy Families (TANF) accounted for roughly .5 percent of the federal budget.[28] Social Security, on the other hand, accounted for roughly 20 percent of the federal budget[29] and Medicare accounted for roughly 16 percent of the federal budget.[30] This is just a partial list of means-tested and social insurance programs, and we see that social insurance programs have a much greater impact on the budget than means-tested programs. Therefore, a true assessment of welfare will involve more than just analyzing the plight of the low-income single parents who receive government assistance or "welfare queens," as they were once derogatorily referred to, but also involves analyzing the plight of seniors, veterans, and many disabled whose primary source of income comes from the federal government.

All three forms of federal government programs have become the sole means of sustenance and survival for many low-income Americans for many years. Along with these programs and policies, Liberalism presents several broader ideas that have been proposed to deal with poverty, which included the Guaranteed Income Movement, strongly advocated in the '60s and '70s and even today, guaranteeing that all Americans working or non-working would have a minimum level of income. There was the argument for Universal Healthcare which was articulated as early as the 1930s by President Roosevelt in his Patients' Bill of Rights and has been a staple in practically every Democratic economic agenda since then. There is the call for reparations, the belief that the government should be held accountable and made to remedy the past acts of economic discriminatory practices that it sanctioned.

Some scholars have attempted to draw distinctions in economic Liberalism between ideas that provide support for those who are disadvantaged and display a willingness to work versus programs that institute entitlement for all regardless of their work ethic or condition of the recipient.

Not all Liberals Think the Same:
Distinctions in Economic Liberalism

Historian Garth Davies contends that there was a major evolution within fiscal Liberalism in terms of addressing poverty. He labels this evolution as the shift from *Opportunity* Liberalism to *Entitlement* Liberalism.[31] The first brand sought to create government programs as a safety net while preserving capitalism.[32] Davies argues that the concept of individualism is not purely a Conservative one, but rather it was a major catalyst behind the creation of the New Deal and Great Society programs.[33] According to Davies, both President Roosevelt and Johnson believed that individualism had to be at the core of any effective Liberal agenda.[34] Liberal programs, according to Davies, helped to increase and expand equal opportunity, hence Opportunity Liberalism.[35]

Davies argues that the shift in Liberalism toward "Entitlement" was a direct result of the many social changes that were taking place in America during the sixties.[36] In this view, race was one in a series of factors that led to this transition. Racial justice, according to Davies, quickly became linked to economic justice.[37] In order to address these changing views, according to Davies, Liberalism shifted from its individualistic tradition and began to create economic programs that did not place such a strong emphasis on personal accountability and responsibility.

Davies' argument is in many ways based upon the deserving and undeserving poor debate with subtle hints of race-based reasoning. Davies' criticism of entitlement Liberalism and praise for opportunity Liberalism presupposes that massive government spending and intervention is plausible and at times necessary to address certain economic conditions. If then the major differences between the two liberal approaches are rooted in their dispositions (deserving and/or undeserving) toward the recipients and the construct of the social programs to hinder or encourage employment, then it would appear that in either scenario the government still has taken ownership of their responsibility to address poverty through massive spending.

The current presidential Administration provides a solid case study in Liberalism across all genres and is in many ways the finest example that we have of overt action by the government in taking ownership for addressing the economy and poverty.

Obamanomics: Keynes, Entitlement, and/or Opportunity Liberalism?

The two major pieces of legislation to come out of the Obama Administration during his first term were the American Recovery and Reinvestment Act (Economic Stimulus Bill) and the Affordable Health Care for America Act (Healthcare Reform Bill). Both of these policies illustrate a renewal of Liberalism in America and serve as President Obama's primary response to poverty.

Keynes in Obamanomics: The American Recovery and Reinvestment Act (Stimulus Bill)

On February 17, 2009, President Obama signed into law the American Recovery and Reinvestment of Act of 2009, frequently referred to as the Stimulus Bill. This bill, which had a record appropriation of $787 billion[38], was, in the words of President Obama, "the most sweeping economic recovery package in our history."[39] The term "sweeping," was very fitting in that the bill attempted to address several areas at the same time and was one of the largest supplemental government appropriations in the history of our country.[40]

But even despite this massive government intervention, it was clear that this bill, and more broadly the economic philosophy that produced the bill, could only provide short-term solutions and was extremely wide in scope. Government stimulus plans do just that: they give the economy a jolt or stimulus which is intended for short-term gains. Increasing funding for entitlement programs or infrastructure does not bring in permanent full-time jobs but rather provides a short-term solution. A year after the bill was passed; there were many Americans who still felt the impact of the recession. The president affirmed these sentiments on the one-year anniversary of signing the bill into law when he stated, "Millions of Americans are still without jobs. Millions more are struggling to make ends meet. It doesn't feel like much of a recovery. I understand that."[41] In 2010, the unemployment rate stayed close to 10 percent throughout the entire year and for nearly all of 2011, the rate has been around 9 percent,[42] which is higher than the 8 percent that the Administration projected for the unemployment rate if the stimulus bill were passed.[43] Many economists on the Left and Right agreed that if the bill were not passed, our country may have fallen into a depression.[44] This bill still begs some questions:

☛ **Points of Reflection:**

If a $787 billion stimulus can only provide short-term solutions, then is the problem outside of the scope of government intervention?

Should a more long-term approach have been taken?

Was stimulating the economy the answer?

While the stimulus bill was indeed an example of very active and aggressive government that addressed more short-term needs, the president's second major policy accomplishment arguably created an even more aggressive and active government.

Patient protection and Affordable Care Act (Health Care Reform)

March 23, 2010, was a major milestone in an almost seventy-year journey to reform the healthcare system in America and to provide coverage for many Americans. The Patient Protection and Affordable Care Act was arguably the most aggressive piece of domestic legislation in the last three decades in terms of federal reform, oversight, and mandates associated with the healthcare. This bill provided tax credits to the middle class in order to defray medical costs, mandated that all plans have free preventative care, increased the reporting process to address medical disparities, and several other measures to address the challenges in the healthcare system.[45] The most debated component of the legislation, which was challenged and eventually affirmed by the United States Supreme Court in 2012, was the government mandate that citizens carry insurance if they were in an economic position to do so; if not they would be subject to a penalty.[46] Here again we find the federal government using stiff regulation, mandates, and fines to regulate the public and private sector and to fund these changes. According to the Congressional Budget Office, which was Democratically controlled, the healthcare bill will produce a $143 billion net reduction in the federal deficit over a ten year period.[47] This reduction will be achieved through increased taxes on higher income citizens and a series of fees and penalties to help offset the cost. This is another tenant of modern Liberalism: increasing government revenues through higher taxes and increased fees to pay for expansive entitlement programs

The Liberal position has strongly advocated the idea that those with the greater resources bear the greatest burden for those who are poor. Many who hold this philosophy focus on meeting the needs regardless of the costs. But even in spite of increased entitlement spending and regulation, some contend that this bill does very little for the poor and is more focused on the middle class. Specifically, it lacked a public option or government sponsored insurance plan similar to Medicare. Others were upset because this reform bill did not cover all residents of America: there were no measures of the bill that provided coverage for illegal immigrants.

In other words, some on the far left in America advocate that this health care bill establishes that most of the policies of the president and modern Liberalism have not been targeted at poverty, but rather the middle class.

Obamanomics: More Focused on the Middle Class and Less on Poverty?

To the impoverished, 2008 and 2009 are no different than 1998 and 1999. Whether most Americans are with or without work, whether interest rates double or decrease, and with or without a housing crisis, there are many Americans who have never owned a home and have resided in poverty for generations regardless of the economic condition of the middle class. The 1990s saw the expansion and direct political targeting by the left toward the middle class. Bill Clinton's success and economic legacy was built upon his direct targeting of the middle class, his departure from fiscal progressivism, and his support of the growing contingency in the Democratic Party of more fiscally moderate Democrats. It was this contingency that supported universal healthcare in 1993, which proposed a government sponsored healthcare plan for the poor, and then, as somewhat of an ideological oxymoron, also supported welfare reform in 1996 which was rooted in removing the poor from the welfare system. On the one hand the argument was made that the government should step in and provide basic health insurance for poor people; on the other hand the argument was made that the government should back away from subsidizing poor people. This blend of entitlement spending coupled with personal responsibility is the essence of what Davies considers "opportunistic policies." During this time the Democrat party moved further and further from the left and closer to the center. One can arguably place President Obama in this mold, with the argument that his policies are more focused on the middle class and less about poverty.[48] There are many on the political Right that think President Obama has done too much entitlement spending and too much for the poor in terms of direct appropriations, while there are progressives on the political left that think the president has abandoned the poor. These two extreme positions may make a strong case that the president has become fiscally moderate with a focus more on the middle class.

Arguably, if the economy over the last decade was not having such a major impact on the middle class, then there would not have been a Stimulus Bill. President Obama's polices, as with many of the recent Democratic presidents, have arguably fit into this mold of blending accountability with massive entitlement spending:

- Mandating that more employers cover their employees with healthcare.

- Imposing penalties on citizens who refuse to acquire health insurance if they have the means to do so.

- Government subsidized refinanced packages for home-owners who are at a risk of foreclosure.

- Increased Pell Grants for college students.

These entitlement policies benefit homeowners, college students, and those employed; all of which are parts of the middle class. But despite the president's support for the middle class, it is difficult to see past the massive spending and accumulation of debt under the current Administration, which makes a strong case that the president is strongly committed to entitlement spending on a level far superior than some of his most recent predecessors.

Obamanomics: Another Leg in the "Unending" Entitlement Marathon?

Practically all of the modern presidents have embraced elements of enti-tlement spending during their terms. A clear example is Social Security. Despite various reforms, each of the presidents has continued to preserve Social Security, the most expensive entitlement program in the federal budget—and it continues to grow. So, in that sense, all of the presidents, both Liberal and Conservative, have run a leg in the "entitlement mara-thon." However, in the case of our current president, he has displayed this same level of commitment to a variety of other programs in addition to Social Security, which led some to believe that his polices and vision for America is the most fiscally leftward leaning that we have had since President Lyndon Baines Johnson's War on Poverty in the 1960s.

President Obama's commitment to massive government spending has frustrated many Americans and led to a resurgence of fiscal Conservatism in America. While the Left has maintained that the government should be an intermediary in addressing poverty, the Right has taken the opposite perspective.

☛ **Point of Reflection:**

Poverty from the Right: Is Too Much Government the Problem?

For the better part of the last thirty years, fiscal Conservatism has been the dominant economic philosophy in our country. There have been regular appeals to "shrink the size of government," "stop subsidizing laziness," "encourage self-responsibility," "promote accountability," and "preserve capitalism." So what we are presently seeing in America is a Conservative resurgence. This resurgence is primarily rooted in anger and frustration toward the Obama Administration and Congress's very aggressive government spending and oversight in America's domestic affairs. While volumes can be written about the role of what has become known as fiscal Conservatism and its impact on society, my question revolves around how Conservatism attempts to address poverty and whether less government is better than more government?

The Roots of Fiscal Conservatism: Poverty Addressed Through Osmosis: "Natural Liberty" (Adam Smith's Invisible Hand)

In 1776, the same year that America gained its independence from Great Britain, there was a major renaissance in economics. In this year, a Scottish professor published his work (that he spent over a decade researching, lecturing, and preparing) on the dynamics of how wealth was accumulated, maintained, and distributed in nations and its impact on governments, businessmen, and, most importantly, ordinary people. The treatise, which was over 1000 pages long and divided into five books, was titled an *Inquiry into the Wealth of Nations*. While Adam Smith's ideas were broad in scope in this study, the most lasting legacy from Smith's work was his belief that wealth would be equitably distributed through a natural evolution, an unintended phenomena what he labeled as an "Invisible Hand."[49] This was a concept Smith first introduced in one of his earliest writings, *The Theory of Moral Sentiments*.[50] The invisible hand was the belief that through the course of individuals pursuing their own economic self-interests, there would be a natural and equitable distribution of wealth, goods, and services among all citizens. In Smith's paradigm, healthy competition would produce equality. Smith famously argued in *The Wealth of Nations*:

> It is not from the benevolence of the butcher, the brewer, or the banker, that we expect our dinner, but from their regard to their own interest. We address ourselves, not to their humanity, but to their self love, and never talk to them of our own necessities but of their advantageous.[51]

Smith's body of work was geared toward the necessity and plight of the common working man, and his idea of an invisible hand was to show that their interests were best addressed in an environment that was based on economic freedom with very minimal government intervention or regulation.[52] Smith believed that a society with these principles, characterized by competition in the market place, would produce a net benefit to society and give an advantage to workers.[53] Smith's primary interest was in establishing an equitable society for the poor or common man, whom he acknowledged made up the mass of society and whose needs it was important to address. According to Smith,

> No society can surely be flourishing and happy, of which the far greater part of the members are poor and miserable.[54]

When reviewing Smith's ideas from the vantage point of twenty-first century economics, it is hard to find the novelty in his concepts. When looking at the different expressions of fiscal Conservatism over the past decades and centuries, most are inundated with Smith's concepts, which are rooted in commitment to the private sector and have great disdain for a massive interventionist government.

Milton Friedman and the Reagan Revolution

Economist Milton Friedman was a former student and advocate of Keynes ideas who later became a player in leading the resurgence of fiscal Conservatism in the '70s and '80s. He helped to usher in a revival of Smith's ideas centuries later. Friedman was an advisor to President Ronald Reagan and was in many ways responsible for Reagan's brand of Conservatism, which championed individualism, minimizing government, and reduced taxes. Friedman argued against any form of government coercion, and he advocated a system of natural liberty that was based upon "uniformity without conformity."[55] Friedman argued that economic freedom was a means toward achieving political freedom.[56] He argued that although mandates from government may benefit the masses, he had concerns about any restrictions on personal freedom or decision making as expressed in many entitlement programs.[57]

Friedman, like Adam Smith, argued for a very limited government overall, and particularly in the context of economic and fiscal matters. Friedman advocated that the government have a role in addressing poverty via a negative income tax, which President Reagan would go on to champion and expand in America.

The Negative Income Tax:
A Conservative Tool to Address Poverty

Friedman advocated the negative income tax as a primary tool to address poverty. The negative Income tax is a tax system where workers who are below the poverty line receive subsidies from the government as opposed to paying taxes. He was generally against most government entitlement programs to the poor.[58] Friedman argues that the negative income tax helps to supplement income by providing a floor for all residents that would be far less costly than typical government welfare programs.[59] While Friedman does point out the issue of taxing some people higher to pay for subsidies for lower income employees, he also points out that there is no real way of completely avoiding this, just reducing it in degrees.[60]

When Ronald Reagan became president, he significantly expanded a version of negative income tax, via Earned Income Tax Credits (EITC), which provides subsidies for working poor people. President Reagan went as far as calling the Earned Income Tax Credit, "the best anti-poverty, the best pro-family, the best job creation measure to come out of Congress of the United States."[61] In this plan, the tax credits would reduce tax liabilities for low-income residents. For some low-income employees, the tax credits would exceed the liabilities, which would be payable to the worker in the form of a refund check. In some respects, this is another form of general assistance or government welfare in that many Americans receive federal tax refunds almost exclusively due to the subsidies, which are direct federal monetary payments. Here the government has a role in addressing poverty, but on a limited basis. Any additional support would have to come via private charities, which many Conservatives believe are more effective than the government.

☛ **Point of Reflection:**

Can the private sector do a better job than the public?

What draws equal amounts of praise and frustration about strict fiscal Conservatism is the strong and almost unapologetic belief in the benefits of the private sector with little to no government intervention. These debates have been played out in education with the discussion of school vouchers and public versus private funding for education and even more so in the recent debates concerning healthcare, pensions, and retirement.

This public versus private debate has been the driving force behind the development of the Tea Party.

The Tea Party

Almost out of nowhere a multi-generational and geographic group of strongly ideological fiscal Conservatives known as the Tea Party has arrived and completely dominated political discussion in almost every circle for much of 2009 and 2010. Prior to the 2008 election, there was not even a mention of a Tea Party, a Tea Party Express, Tea Party Nation, or Ensuring Liberty (Tea Party PAC) in political discussion; but as of the mid-term elections of 2010, the debt ceiling debate of 2011, and the early months of the 2012 presidential elections, this group is largely responsible for the major shift that has taken place in Washington, DC, and in several states around the country. During the first two years of the Obama Administration up through the mid-term elections, this group is by far one of the most influential and pivotal groups in American politics today.

What is clear about the composition of the Tea Party is that they represent a group of people that come from various backgrounds and economic stratums who are frustrated with the massive spending by the federal government and they appear to be very unapologetic in their very aggressive and confrontational tactics in supporting their beliefs.

The Tea Party: What Do They Stand For?

Since this organization is not an official party, they do not have a political platform, but rather most of their beliefs hinge on three fundamental principles:[62]

- Lower taxes

- Limited government

- More individual freedom

Much of the rhetoric that takes place during Tea Party events focuses on these three ideas. This movement really does not delve into marrying these ideas to specific policies, but rather they are rooted in building support based on advancing broad-based theme principles. For example, there was strong support from the Tea Party for the Americans for Tax Reform Pledge that categorically does not support raising the marginal tax rate *for any reason*.[63] The Tea Party has also positioned themselves as being very strong critics of President Obama's fiscal policy, largely because of the president's support for raising the debt ceiling, increased entitlements spending, and support for government bailouts; all are fiscal policies that previous Democrats and Republican presidents have each supported. The Tea Party has built a coalition based upon imagery, ideas, and rhetoric to gain a massive following of ideologues fiscal Conservatives.

Although the Tea Party does argue that government should be curtailed, they are not of the belief that is should be absolved, as does Libertarianism in America. Libertarians support the total elimination of all government social programs, as defined in their national platform:

> We should eliminate the entire social welfare system. This includes eliminating AFDC, food stamps, subsidized housing, and all the rest. Individuals who are unable to fully support themselves and their families through the job market must, once again, learn to rely on supportive family, church, community, or private charity to bridge the gap.[64]

Fiscally the Tea Party supports a very limited government and sees the role of the government as strengthening morality as a means to address poverty or economic challenges in our culture.

Distinctions in Conservatism: Small Government Does Not Mean No Government

Poverty Mended Through Morality

As discussed in Question 1, there is a contingent of fiscal Conservatives that want the government to stay out of their pockets; but when it comes to issues such as the legalization of drugs, abortion rights, and gay marriage, many Conservatives are quick to point out that government should be in place and strongly enforce policies that restrict or hinder these activities. Libertarians, who are also fiscally moderate and are to the Right of Conservatives on the role of government, seek no government intervention even on these non-fiscal matters as well. The distinctions in Conservatism on the role of government really, for the most part, hinge on the marriage between money and morality or faith and economics. Most modern Conservatives fit into this hybrid model of Conservatism. This model has dominated the media with the belief that good behavior, ethical decisions, morality in the home, and a strong faith community can and should be in place and will serve as a remedy for many of the economic challenges in our society.

In 1996 when the Conservative Congress led by former House Speaker Newt Gingrich drafted the Personal Responsibility and Work Opportunity Reconciliation Act of 1996 (Welfare Reform Act), the first lines of the bill read like Sunday morning sermon notes. It stated:

> Marriage is the foundation of a successful society. Marriage is an essential institution of a successful society, which promotes the interest of children. Promotion of responsible fatherhood and motherhood is integral to successful child rearing and the well-being of children.[65]

This bill was a referendum on welfare and government subsidies; however, it began with a lecture on the necessities of strong families. According to this ideology, it is the mix of morality and faith that leads to strong economic stability. As indicated in Question 1, African Americans hold very strong views in regards to the role of faith in politics;[66] however, also as indicated in Question 1, African Americans still believe that the government should be more assertive in addressing poverty.[67] This belief has led to the strenuous relationship between African Americans and fiscal Conservatism over the past four to five decades.

African Americans and Fiscal Conservatism

There are many reasons to explain the low level of support by African Americans toward fiscal Conservative policies on a more aggregate level. First, there is a common belief among African Americans that the federal government should answer fiscal challenges in society, as expressed through much of African and American history. Secondly, many African Americans have grown weary of the perceived lack of empathy and disdain for the less affluent and impoverished in America that is associated with limited government. Again, even though many African Americans support the belief in each individual having primary personal responsibility for his/her own economic well-being, they still believe in a federal government that has some concern for the less affluent and that will at times respond to major economic challenges in our culture. A good case study of this tension is an example that Milton Friedman offers in his book *Capitalism and Freedom*.

> For example consider a situation in which there are grocery stores serving a neighborhood inhabited by people who have a strong aversion to being waited on by Negro clerks. Suppose one of the grocery stores has a vacancy for a clerk and the first applicant qualified in other respects happens to be a Negro. Let us suppose that as a result of the law, the store is required to hire him. The effect of this action will be to reduce the business done by this store and to impose losses on the owner. If the preference of the community is strong enough, it may even cause the store to close. When the owner of the store hires white clerks in preference to Negroes, in the absence of the law, he may not be expressing any preference or prejudice or taste of his own. He may simply be transmitting the taste of the community. He is, as it were, producing the services for the consumers that the consumers are willing to pay for. Nonetheless, he is harmed, and indeed may be the only one harmed appreciably, by a law which prohibits him from pandering to the tastes of the community for having a white rather than a Negro clerk. The consumers, whose preferences the law is intended to curb, will be affected substantially only to the extent that the number of stores is limited and hence they must pay higher prices because one store has gone out of business.[68]

While the store owner may not be prejudiced or racist in his refusal to hire the Negro, the concern rises with the clear absence of moral law being blended with individual freedom. The scenario discusses a highly qualified Negro. It is one thing if the discussion was in regards to a lesser qualified applicant, but to deny hiring to a highly qualified applicant due to racial preferences of a community breeds a culture of segregation and separatism if a community so desires. While this scenario was presented in the early '60s, even today prominent politicians like United States Senator Rand Paul share similar views with Milton Friedman in regards to this issue; with Senator Paul indicating his opposition for the landmark Civil Rights Act of 1965, and the idea of the federal government telling business that they could not discriminate.[69]

The belief that a political party or ideology is unconcerned and completely indifferent toward the plight of the impoverished and that a party or belief system is so committed to an ideological belief on government that it would indirectly support racism and discrimination has led to the deep divisions between many African Americans and the Republican Party. And in turn this has facilitated the massive acceptance of the Democratic Party by African Americans, despite the many ideological differences that exist between the majority of African Americans and social Liberalism, as expressed in Question 1. Many fiscal Conservatives may make the case that they are indeed concerned about the poor, but just do not see the government as the solution. It does not help their argument when in 2012, Republican candidate for president Governor Mitt Romney said, "I'm in this race because I care about Americans. I'm not concerned about the very poor. We have a safety net there. If it needs repair, I'll fix it."[70] In his entire statement he argued his support for the middle class and how he was also not concerned with the *very rich*. This overt disdain for the poor is one in a series of events that have kept many African Americans away from fiscal Conservatism, as articulated by those who carry this perspective.

Possibly, the issue for many African Americans does not come down to the legislative track record of both political parties, but arguably the cleavages are based more on tone, perception, and image rather than pure ideology. If the issue was a matter of policies and legislative record, what we find from both parties is not strict Conservatism or Liberalism in terms of their policies; but we do find strict Conservatism and Liberalism in regards to their rhetoric. Despite what has been said, history shows us that both parties have been willing to deviate from their core ideological backgrounds in order to do what was best for each particular moment in time.

Each of the Recent Democrat and Republican Presidents Have Embraced Fiscal Compromise

☛ **Point of Reflection:**

Fiscally, does compromise reflect an impediment or indicator of convictions?

What we have seen in recent history has been a shift toward fiscal moderation. Most of the recent presidents took an economic path that they considered to be best for the economic conditions during their time in office, even if it was antithetical to their campaign jargon or personal and political ideology. Most recent presidents have done something to address poverty and this course has taken them down the path of moderation. This is a trend that I believe we have seen from both Conservative and Liberal presidents.

Ronald Reagan

Ronald Reagan is in many ways the finest example that we have of deviation from campaign and ideological rhetoric in addressing the social needs of his time. Reagan was a Conservative Republican president who campaigned on shrinking the size of government and eliminating the department of education and who used jargon such as "welfare bums" and "welfare queens" to express his staunch criticism of government subsidies of supposed laziness. When comforted with economic challenges and high unemployment rates during his presidency, he supported a program that was a form of welfare spending: Earned Income Tax Credits. *While President Reagan is also best known for his massive tax cuts, the president did not cut many of the major social programs such as food stamps or general assistance; nor did he close the Department of Education as he had promised. Reagan consistently spoke out against these programs, but he did very little in terms of actually cutting them.*

George H. W. Bush

George Herbert Walker Bush, a moderate Conservative Republican president, ran for office in 1988 with a bold campaign promise: "Read my lips, no new taxes." However, in 1990 when the nation was facing a serious budget deficit, the president convened a series of talks with leaders of both parties, appealed to the American people, and convened a "deficit reduction plan" that led him to agree to raising taxes for the betterment of the economy. These taxes included tax increases for the rich, which was a Conservative no-no.[71] While he personally opposed this policy, he believed it needed to be done for the betterment of the economy.

Bill Clinton

We can look at President Bill Clinton, a Leftward-leaning Democrat, whose success as a president came when he signed a Balanced Budget Act of 1997 and he supported the Welfare Reform Act. This later ended AFDC as it had been known for decades and replaced it with the time limited program TANF. TANF made serious cuts in entitlement spending and placed major limitations on general assistance. These steps were more drastic in terms of reforming entitlement spending than what was done by the previous two Republican Administrations. This decision was strongly opposed by many on the political Left who were seen as some of President Clinton's core supporters.

George W. Bush

George W. Bush was a Conservative Republican president whose first major policy initiative was a massive tax cut for all Americans and a few years later he expanded socialized medicine via Medicare Part D (pre-scription drug program) which offered government subsidies. Then, by the end of his presidency, he signed into law the Troubled Asset Relief Program (TARP) where the federal government bought assets in several major companies to address the severe economic challenges the nation was facing. One of the largest programs to come out of TARP was the government purchasing troubled mortgages and securing assets of many financial institutions. TARP would be referred to as a bank bailout bill and was the largest infusion by the federal government into the private sector. Although the bill was signed during Bush's second term, he still alienated the far right wing of his party. Arguably, this bill was the cause of the Conservative uprising which is seen in the Tea Party.

Barack Obama

President Obama, a Liberal Democratic, first signed into law the largest Stimulus Bill in American history and then extended the Bush Tax Cuts for an additional two years, which was the largest tax cut in the history of the country. In many ways there is no ideological pattern or synergy to his economic policies, which has drawn great criticism from the Left and the Right.

What we have seen from each of the above mentioned leaders was a commitment to transcend an established economic philosophy to address the needs that were most pressing for their generation. While these decisions led to some of the leaders not being reelected, some losing majorities in Congress, some receiving very low approval ratings, and each receiving some criticism from the staunch ideologues in their parties, I think it is comfortable to say that each embraced elements of compromise to address the issues facing their generation, which in some way extended to the poor.

While each of the presidents and political parties have responded to issues and elements of poverty differently through their rhetoric and policies, at the end of the day I think we would be hard pressed to find a Democrat, Republican, Liberal, or Conservative elected official who has established through a political or policy track record a desire of taking direct ownership for remedying poverty by means of government. While some speak on the subject matter with great passion, there still is a great challenge with finding a belief or practice that places direct ownership for remedying poverty primarily in the hands of government.

Ownership would involve more than making good speeches and providing marginal sustenance to certain groups of people. Ownership would mean a universal, all-inclusive, sustained effort by government to address the economic challenges of all of the poor. Such a plan would include defining clear objectives for the poor, and if success is not reached, then continuing to make efforts and taking direct action until the disease of poverty has been cured. This is what would be involved with government ownership of poverty. The scope of that type of undertaking would lead one to believe that if government will not or cannot take on this challenge, then quite possibly the solution or ownership for addressing poverty may rest with each individual.

☞ **Point of Reflection:**

Self-accountability: Are the impoverished responsible for their own predicament?

One of the common misnomers about success and/or successful people is the belief that success—whether occupational, academic, physical, or financial—is somehow equated with unethical behavior, having some exclusive advantage, or having some hidden asset. The belief that hard work, tenacity, planning, and diligence in and of itself is enough to overcome major obstacles has somewhat been supplanted with the idea that "my plight is someone else's problem." This phenomenon has led to the almost complete repudiation of the idea that ownership for addressing poverty may quite possibly rest with the impoverished themselves. *While it must be noted that ownership by one party does not absolve others from responsibility,* ownership does answer the question at the end of the day about who has primary responsibility and who should be held accountable?

When poverty is seen as an incurable, debilitating, and paralyzing disease, then it would be insane at best to expect invalids to liberate themselves. However, when poverty is seen as a sickness or temporary state of discomfort that one has the ability to control, then the idea of direct ownership for one's own plight becomes not just a reality but a necessity. The unfortunate plight of the impoverished has been a front row seat to watch the church and government grapple over when and how poverty should be addressed, with anticipation that their hopes and destiny are tied to a government program, outreach effort, or an act of piety to meet their needs.

In some respects, the idea of self-accountability and ownership can best be equated with socialization and worldview. This was the paradigm used by Booker T. Washington many years ago. His principles on liberation were hewed in a time period of great challenge and transition in America, which makes his ideas relevant and contemporary for the challenges of today.

Booker T. Washington: Revolution and Liberation through Self-Accountability, Hard Work, and Establishing Capital

> Success is to be measured not so much by the position that one has reached in life…as by the obstacles which he has overcome while trying to succeed.
> —BOOKER T. WASHINGTON

As a man who transitioned from life as a slave to serving as an established entrepreneur and renowned university president, Booker T. Washington had the academic background and personal experience to speak about the necessities of self-accountability and taking direct ownership for one's plight in the face of the greatest adversity that any human being could face: slavery.

Washington was raised during the years of the Reconstruction where many of the former slaves were now being educated via programs created by the Freedmen's Bureau. Washington's worldview on economics and empowerment were developed during his time at Hampton Normal and Agricultural Institute (now Hampton University) where he was strongly influenced by the educational philosophy of Samuel Anderson who was founder and president of the University. Anderson stressed that students not only receive educational training in teaching but that students also receive training in manual labor and technical skills so that they would develop as well-rounded students, use their skills to help pay for their own education, and most importantly, develop the skills of self-reliance and personal responsibility during these very formative years.[72]

At Hampton, Anderson became very pleased with Washington, referring to him as, "the most perfect specimen of man, physically, mentally and spiritually the most Christ-like."[73] After Washington completed his studies at Hampton and then later at Wayland Seminary (later Virginia Union University), he was asked by Anderson to come back as an instructor at Hampton. Later, at the young of age of twenty-six, he was recommended by Anderson to be the first leader at Tuskegee Institute in Alabama, a school that was being formed with many of the same principles as Hampton University.

Liberation through self-help and an entrepreneurial mindset

Washington's legacy and contribution to American history is rooted in his experiences, ideas, and philosophy that he implemented during his lifelong commitment to establishing Tuskegee University. Washington's ideas were to teach students the principles of self-help and self-responsibility through integrating their classroom studies with manual labor to help students develop skills that would give them the ability to make a way for themselves and take accountability for their lives. One such experiment was having the students build the dormitory that they were going to live in. Washington argued the following: "But that in the teaching of civilization, self-help and self reliance, the erection of the building by the students themselves would more than compensate for any lack of comfort or fine finish."[74]

Washington believed that through individual hard work and responsibility students could develop the skills and discipline to put them in demand, even in a society that looked at Blacks as being inferior. Washington talked about another experience he had with teaching the students to build bricks that could be sold in the market place:

> Many White people who had no contact with the school, and per-
> haps no sympathy with it, came to us to buy bricks because they
> found out that ours were good bricks. They discovered that we were
> supplying a real want in the community.[75]

These revolutionary lessons that Washington instilled gave African
Americans the ability and capacity to control their future through implementing the ideas of self-responsibility, ownership, and establishing capital in an oppressive culture.

Washington was a practitioner who believed that hard work and diligence had the power to transcend racism.[76]

☞ **Points of Reflection:**

> *Can excellence, diligence, and the accumulation of capital eradi-
> cate racism?*

> *Can excellence, diligence, and the accumulation of capital sup-
> plant racism?*

More practically:

☞ **Point of Reflection:**

> *Are Oprah, Michael Jordan, or President Obama primarily seen
> as being successful or primarily seen as being African American?*

Making Right Decisions: Is College the Answer to Poverty?

While Washington himself was trained and prepared to be a teacher at
both Hampton Institute and Wayland Seminary and would later go on
to put in place teacher training at Tuskegee, his idea was to blend elements of textbook training with practical training to increase each student's marketability and to give students the skills to better themselves.
Washington did not completely shun textbook education or theoretical
training, but he was very critical of the abundance of faith that many of
the former slaves placed in it, while not coupling formal education with
training that he believed would make individual success more of a reality.
In response to the belief among students about the benefits of formal
textbook training, Washington argued,

> The idea, however, was too prevalent that as soon as one secured
> a little education, in some unexplainable way he would be free

from most of the hardships of the world, and at any rate, could live without manual labor.[77]

Washington's assessment was not so much avid support for manual labor as it was his massive support for establishing capital and building skills so that his students would be in the best position to take responsibility and ownership for their well-being. On a broader level, Washington's position was geared toward choosing an educational path that would render the highest probability of becoming self-sufficient.

These ideas reminded me of a conversation I had with some friends after finishing college. We each studied hard and successfully made it through our undergraduate education. Many went on to graduate school and some on to other professional schools. However, a common thread among the group was that after finishing college, there was not a preponderance of job offers or opportunities available. While on the one hand this shortage could be attributed to the challenging economic times we were in, on the other hand our frustration could also be equated to the unrealistic expectations that are placed in exclusively receiving a college degree. From the time that children are born, there is an expectation that you should go to college and that by doing so you will position yourself for a good future. This mindset has led to the belief that the world will be at your fingertips when you walk across the stage and get the degree. Unfortunately, for many Americans this has not been a reality. In this chapter there have been discussions about the poor and the working poor, but we must also look at the college educated poor.

☛ **Point of Reflection:**

Is it really possible to be college educated and have a bachelors, masters, or doctorate degree and be economically poor?

As a college graduate, I can certainly attest to the many benefits of receiving a college education. I have in the past and will continue to strongly encourage others to do the same and support universities. However, if each individual is responsible for his/her own future, then realistic planning and preparation made for life after school and preparation made for one's economic future is mandatory. In the African American community, going to college and getting a degree has always been the clear image of making smart and intelligent decisions about your future, while at the same time the necessity of financial and economic education has remained faint at best. A reality in America today is that a person may spend anywhere from four to six years in undergraduate education and then spend the next twenty years repaying that education while working in a job that only pays enough to meet minimum living standards, living from paycheck to paycheck. In 2008 "nearly 60 percent of low-income young adults were attending or earned a credential from a postsecondary institution during this time."[78]

College education may indeed be one in a series of vehicles to financial freedom, but it would appear that college education or any other form of formal training ought to be coupled with financial literacy or some form of training that provides opportunities to sustain oneself.

In Conclusion

So as I think back to the man whom I saw in the supermarket that evening, I wonder what was the reason for him stealing food? Was it because the government did not provide enough assistance? Because churches were not as aggressive in addressing his needs? Did he make bad decisions? There probably is not an all-inclusive answer. How he gets out of that predicament is the question that deserves our attention. I could attempt to answer the question. Society could attempt to answer it. Philosophers, pastors, and politicians could attempt to answer it. However, the most important answer would be the answer that comes directly from him.

Question 4

HOMOSEXUALITY IN AMERICA: IS AFRICAN AMERICAN SYNONYMOUS WITH GAY AMERICAN?

A S AN UNDERGRADUATE at Virginia State University, I served as a resident assistant from my sophomore year to my senior year. Prior to classes starting each year, the university offered training to the resident assistants. One year the training was held at Virginia Commonwealth University in Richmond, Virginia, with many other RA's from neighboring universities in attendance. On this particular occasion, the topic at our training session was *diversity*. After a few minutes of listening to the facilitator during the training session, it became very obvious that the facilitator was homosexual and that this presentation on *diversity* was really a presentation on the need for society to accept, respect, and have compassion on the gay and lesbian lifestyles.

During the presentation, the facilitator shared her life story and how she made the evolution from being quiet, or "in the closet," to eventually coming out of the closet and being a champion for gay and lesbian rights. In telling her story, she talked about growing up in the church, playing sports in high school, going through puberty, discovering her sexual identity, and some of the other challenging experiences that she had on her journey. She shared how leaders should create a friendly environment for all people. The facilitator went on to explain how she was a Christian and loved the Lord her whole life and how she reconciled being a Christian with being gay. She went on to express her strong criticism for comments and actions made by two nationally known Virginia ministers in their dissent of homosexuality. At the conclusion of the presentation, the facilitator asked, "Are there any questions"? Before she could get the "Are there," out of her mouth, my hand went up in the air, and I asked:

"During your presentation, I noticed that you made several references to the Bible. Are you implying that the Bible validates homosexual behavior?"

She responded, "Many of the scriptures in the Bible that speak against gay and lesbians are outdated; those same scriptures forbid the eating of shellfish such as crabs, shrimps, and lobsters."

I responded, "Respectfully, ma'am, we are not talking about seafood; we are talking about the Bible supporting gay rights."

She went on to explain that God was a loving God and that He was concerned about all people and that we should not judge one another.

Pretty soon, all the room became quiet as the conversation shifted to a dialogue between her, the presenter, and the outspoken, inquisitive student, me. I asked her if she believed it was possible to still love and respect a person and not agree or sanction their actions.

She understood that my questioning was rooted in a biblical dissent. She went on to explain that she grew up in a fun-loving Christian home with both parents, had a normal childhood, but was a tom-boy growing up and increasingly found that she was not attracted to men.

When the presentation was over, we continued our discussion further, gave each other a hug, and went our separate ways. I must admit, I was shocked; that was my first time but would not be my last time in life hearing someone attempt to use Scripture to validate homosexuality. It was also around this same time that I began to see how homosexuality was sweeping through all facets of the American culture at a very rapid pace.

Homosexuality in America: The Cultural Question of this Generation

In many ways this discourse that I had with the facilitator was indicative of the many issues surrounding homosexuality in America in our present culture. Here we were in a public institution with a diverse student body, primarily African Americans, talking about the role of homosexuality in education, in the Bible, in race, and the acceptance or rejection by others of homosexuality. Discourse on this level was, in many ways, unique to this generation.

Every generation in American history has cultural questions that they must answer in terms of redefining American life and values. In the '50s and '60s, the cultural question facing that generation was the evolving role of African Americans in all facets of the American culture. In the '70s and '80s the question facing that generation was the evolving role of women in the American culture. For the last fifteen or so years, the focus has shifted to homosexuality in America. In previous generations homosexuality was not seen as a mainstream issue. Most gays and lesbians remained "in the closet," so most political, cultural, or religious circles did not have to address this issue in detail. However, in this generation things have changed. In many respects, homosexuality has evolved from a side issue, to arguably the greatest cultural issue or question that this generation must deal with.

Prior to the 2004 election, I was discussing issues with two close Christian friends regarding what was going to determine their decision on Election Day. One of my friends stated that the most important issue was the economy, while the other friend said that the most important issue to him was surrounding gay rights and how they were influencing the society. My friend who advocated the economy told the other friend that gay and lesbian rights were not that big of a deal and that jobs, the economy, and poverty were more significant than a person's private sex life. Around the same time, I was watching a cable news network (MSNBC) and heard Rev. Al Sharpton make a comment in regards to gay rights and jobs. He said, "It does not matter who you sleep with, as long as you have a job when you wake up."

The comment by Rev. Sharpton and conversation by my friends left two impressions. First, it was their belief, commonly held by many, that sexual morality and decisions regarding family were not as significant as economic issues and that gay rights were not as relevant to their life as the economy and jobs. These are common beliefs in our generation; but the reality is that every generation in biblical, world, and American history has dealt with economic challenges and economic disagreements. History teaches us that the fiscal challenges that our country is currently going through are indeed important and on some levels will always exist. These economic challenges are by no means exclusive to this generation in the same manner that issues surrounding gay, lesbian, bisexual, and transgender (GLBT) rights are.

The second impression that it left on me was the apparent lack of understanding of how much homosexuality is redefining just about every facet of our culture and how GLBT in America is so much bigger than the issue of gay marriage or domestic partnership. GLBT rights is transforming just about every sector of American society, from politics to the pulpit and everything in between, on a level that other generations have never experienced.

The Rapid Evolution of Homosexuality in America

Homosexuality in athletics

In athletics we have seen Sheryl Swoops, who arguably was the best female basketball player of this generation, come out of the closet. In 2007 former NBA player John Amechi became the first former NBA player to publicly acknowledge that he was gay via his memoir *Man in the Middle*. Later that year another former NBA player, Tim Hardaway, got massive attention for his very candid opposition to homosexuality. In 2010, Kye Allums became the first transgender athlete to play Division I sports when he played for the George Washington University women's basketball team. In late 2011, the leading story in all of the news media, which got just as much attention as the presidential election, was the story surrounding the allegations of pedophilia and homosexual behavior by two former Division 1 college coaches.

Homosexuality in education

In education we have the example of Harvey Milk High School in New York City. This school, which started as a two classroom building in 1985, received its full accreditation in 2002 and is the first publicly funded high school in America which was created for and caters directly to gay and lesbian youth.[1] Since 2002 other cities have explored the possibility of establishing this brand of alternative education. In 2002 the children's book *King and King* was published, which told the story of a prince who gets married to another man. At the end of the book there is an image of both men kissing.[2] This book sparked massive debate around the country and was the cause of a lawsuit in Massachusetts due to it being used in a public school classroom.[3] Also in education, there are many public schools that are debating issues regarding allowing students to cross dress (dress as a member of the opposite sex) on regular class days.

Homosexuality in entertainment

In 1994 Roseanne Arnold was one of the first celebrities to participate in an on air lesbian kiss during her show *Roseanne*. In 2002 Rosie O'Donnell publicly "came out" and became the first openly gay and lesbian daytime talk show host on network television to "come out." Ellen DeGeneres followed in 2003. Also, in 2005 the Logo Network was launched, becoming the first television network that was targeted toward the GLBT community.

QUESTION 4: Homosexuality in America:
Is African American Synonymous with Gay American?

79

Homosexuality in politics

During the 2008 Democratic presidential primary on August 8, 2007, the Logo Network sponsored a debate which was the first presidential debate that focused exclusively on gay and lesbian issues. In previous elections there would be a few questions asked about gay rights, but never before had an entire debate been devoted to the subject. In 1999 the National Stonewall Democrats were founded representing GLBT in the Democratic Party. In 2009 GOProud was founded as a Conservative "527 organization" representing Conservative GLBT issues. GOProud was formed by former members of the Log Cabin Republicans, founded in 1977 in protest against the Briggs Initiative. In addition, when Republican Governor George W. Bush was vetting his potential vice president Dick Cheney, one of the first issues that Cheney brought to Governor Bush was that his daughter was openly homosexual and that he was not in support of a ban on gay marriage. This was an issue that Bush championed and arguably became the catalyst behind his 2004 victory. Then in 2012, President Obama became the first sitting president to openly support gay and lesbian marriage and the Democratic National Committee has recently announced plans to add support for same-sex marriage to its party's national platform.

Homosexuality in the church

Former national evangelical pastor Ted Haggard has been involved in homosexual relationships, gospel music star Tonex has come out of the closet, and *former* Pentecostal Bishop Carlton Pearson and African Bishop Desmond Tutu have been outspoken in their support of homosexuality. In 2005 the United Church of Christ became the largest Christian Organization to allow same-sex marriage when it adopted its "Equal Marriage Rights for All Resolution" at its 25th Synod. In 2003 the Episcopal Church voted to appoint its first gay bishop, and in 2009, at its 76th General Convention, it gave approval for the ordination of other openly gay bishops on a wider scale.[4]

The issue is validation of homosexuality

The issue of this generation is not about people of the same sex having intimate relationships and living and functioning as heterosexual couples. These practices have existed for many years secretly and, as with other practices, will probably continue regardless of any law, statute, or statement by churches. The issue that is unique to this generation is the idea of homosexuality being validated and constantly expanded by the government, churches, and our culture and the degree to which homosexuality is equitable to heterosexuality in culture, faith, and politics. What makes the discussion even more challenging is the growing reality that compromise or a middle ground has become less and less feasible. We find two good case studies that illustrate the challenges of compromise on this issue: gays in the military and gay marriage in America.

Homosexuality in America: Is Compromise Feasible?

Don't Ask Don't Tell and Gay Marriage

When President Clinton came to office in 1993, one of his campaign promises was to end discrimination in the military toward homosexuals and to allow them to openly serve. His Administration drafted a policy that was intended to be a compromise—Department of Defense Directive 1304.26, more commonly referred to as Don't Ask Don't Tell (DADT). This policy made adjustments to the admission criteria in the armed services, which allowed homosexuals to serve in the military as long as they did not reveal or act upon their sexual orientation, with the understanding that they would not be required to reveal their sexual orientation during the admission process.[5]

While the gay and lesbian community was not ecstatic about the legislation because of its obvious hypocrisy, this policy was seen as a major stride toward including gay and lesbians into the armed services. A few years later, in 1996, President Clinton signed into law the Defense of Marriage Act of 1996 (DOMA), which under federal law defined marriage as a union between one man and one woman.[6]

President Clinton's policies in the 1990s were considered to be moderate in terms of gay and lesbian rights. Although he did receive criticism on these issues from the gay and lesbian community, they still supported him and have remained faithful Democrats at large. However, the tenor of the debate has shifted so much in the past ten to fifteen years that it would be considered betrayal for a major leader from the Democratic Party today to support either piece of legislation. The founders of DADT, President Clinton and former Secretary of State Colin Powell, have both spoken out against the policy and have shifted their opinion on legislation that they once supported.[7] Within the past year the pressure from the gay and lesbian community resulted in Congress and President Obama signing into law the Don't Ask Don't Tell Repeal Act of 2010, which put in place policies and a process that currently allows gay and lesbians to openly serve in the military.

In regard to gay marriage, in the aftermath of the 2004 presidential elections, many social Liberals criticized Republican strategist Karl Rove because he worked to place constitutional ballot initiatives on several state ballots that defined marriage as the union between "one man and one woman"; the same language used in the Defense of Marriage Act in the 1990s.[8] What was once acceptable in the '90s has become bigotry and fanaticism in less than decade. Just as with DADT, President Clinton has changed his perspective and has come out with strong support for gay marriage.[9] In addition, President Obama supports a repeal of DOMA and has instructed the attorney general to no longer enforce it on a federal level.[10] President Obama was also very active in fighting for the same sex marriage bill in New York in 2011.

This shift on the political Left from a moderate to an absolute position on this issue illustrates an overall divided America on the subject of gay and lesbian's rights. I found it necessary to do some historical analysis of GLBT rights to get a better understanding of the scope of this issue; and this analysis revealed great similarities to another major social movement in America.

Homosexuality in America: The Moment (Stonewall) and the Mauter (Milk)[11]

On Friday night of June 27 and the early morning hours on June 28, 1969, a group of police officers made one of their frequent raids at a very meager looking mafia-owned gay bar in the Greenwich Village section of New York City. This bar, known as the Stonewall Inn, became a hub and one of the major social scenes for gay men in New York City. The Stonewall Inn attracted gay men, transvestites, drag queens, and underage male homosexuals from various backgrounds, who would come to dance, drink, do drugs, and participate in prostitution with each other.

On almost a monthly basis, officers would come into the club, check IDs, and do an inspection to allegedly make sure that no illegal activities were going on. According to some accounts, these raids were more of a front because the officers were being paid substantially "under the table" by the owners to not shut the bar down. On this particular night, the attendees at the Stonewall became very indignant and refused to cooperate with the officers. What ensued was a massive arrest of many of the patrons who were resisting the police officers and a large restless crowd growing outside of the bar who began throwing bottles, coins, trash cans filled with fire, parking meters, and several other objects at the police officers.

While today this may not seem unique, at the time it was one of the very first aggressive confrontations between homosexuals and police officers. In the following nights, the riots continued and eventually subsided later in the week. The news of the riots began to gain attention locally and around the country with these events becoming the face of the mounting frustration of the gay and lesbian community.

Impact of the Stonewall riots

Prior to the Stonewall riots there were a few social/non-profit activist "homophile organizations," as they were referred to at the time, that were formed to represent the needs of homosexuals around the country:

- In 1924 the short-lived Society for Human Rights

- In 1950 the Mattachine Society was founded by Harry Hay who was an active member of the Communist Party. This organization focused on the political rights of homosexuals. (There are other groups that began to form around the country under the same name.)

- In 1952 One Incorporated was founded. One started as the name of a monthly publication produced by the Mattachine Society, but splintered in 1952 as a result of a split in the Mattachine Society. One Inc would go on to become its own separate organization.

- In 1955 the Daughters of Bilitis was formed as an organization representing the needs of lesbians. They began to produce a monthly publication called *The Ladder Magazine*.

- In 1963 the East Coast Homophile Organizations (ECHO), a conglomerate of gay and lesbian organizations, formed on the East Coast.

QUESTION 4: Homosexuality in America:
Is African American Synonymous with Gay American?

83

- In 1966 North American Conference of Homosexual Organizations (NACHO), a conglomerate of homophile organizations, formed nationwide.

- In July of 1969 the Gay Liberation Front was founded as a more proactive and radical homophile organization. This group used a bald fist as its official logo. Later that year the Gay Activist Alliance was created.

- In commemoration of the Stonewall riots in June 1970, the first anniversary of the event, the Christopher Street Liberation Day March was organized with similar events being held around the country on the same weekend. Eventually the name gay liberation evolved into gay pride and, as of 2012, most major cities in America have a gay pride march to commemorate the Stonewall riots.

- In addition to the riots, the events that took place on the West Coast surrounding the life and subsequent death of a former camera shop owner put a face on the gay and lesbian movement in America.

Harvey Milk and the Castro District[12]

If a bullet should enter my brain, let that bullet destroy every closet door in this country.
—HARVEY MILK, 1978

In the early 1970s, Harvey Milk, a former Navy officer, Wall Street executive, and participant in the anti-war movement, migrated from New York to San Francisco. Once in California, Milk opened a camera shop in a section of town that became one of the major neighborhoods in the country for gays and lesbians: the Castro District. Milk quickly became a community activist in the Castro District and would go on to develop himself as a leading voice for gay and lesbian rights and would be referred to as "Mayor of the Castro District." In 1974 he founded the Castro Street Fair, which was one of the largest gay and lesbian events in the county at the time. In 1976 he founded the San Francisco Gay Democratic Club; and in the fall of 1977, Harvey Milk became the first openly gay person to be elected to a municipal public office in San Francisco and in a large national city when he was elected to the San Francisco Board of Supervisors. He was also very instrumental in getting a gay rights ordinance passed in the city and he was successful in leading a statewide campaign that defeated The Briggs Initiative, a policy that would have banned homosexuals from participating in or advocating for homosexual behavior in public schools.

In November of 1978, a few days after The Briggs Initiate was defeated, one of Harvey Milk's colleagues on the Board of Supervisors named Dan White, who was strongly against the city ordinance in support of homosexuals and who backed The Briggs Initiative, initially resigned from the Board of Supervisors. He later wanted to get back on the board, but was not supported by the mayor, Harvey Milk, or other supervisors. On November 27, 1978, Dan White entered City Hall through a side window and shot and killed both the mayor and Harvey Milk. Milk's life and death would be a major catalyst in the gay and lesbian movement in America for decades to come. In 2009 Sean Penn won an Oscar for Best Actor in his portrayal of Harvey Milk in the 2008 film *Milk,* and later that year President Barack Obama awarded Harvey Milk a Presidential Medal of Freedom posthumously.

The Stonewall Riots and the killing of Harvey Milk were, in many ways, the turning points for the GLBT community. In some respects, these stories sound familiar.

Is Gay American Synonymous with African American or Any Other Minority for That Matter?

Whenever a person or group in America is mistreated, discriminated against, or perceived to be treated unjustly, there is always a tendency to draw comparisons between that group and African Americans. Indeed the story of African Americans is rooted in a history of overcoming discrimination, racism, and systematic exclusion in order to achieve freedom and equality. While this story is by no means exclusively an African American story, what has distinguished the African American freedom struggle is the fact that it involved such a large volume of people, it lasted over a four hundred year time period, and it involved physical, mental, and psychological enslavement for the vast majority of that time. After the physical enslavement ended, there were a body of laws sanctioned by government that mandated overt discrimination and segregation. The African American freedom struggle was rooted in morality, humility, and dignity by the oppressed with the battle being waged on the grounds of faith, religion, and morality.

QUESTION 4: Homosexuality in America:
Is African American Synonymous with Gay American?

85

Some of these attributes were common to other ethnicities, but the totality of these experiences suffered by African Americans will naturally draw parallels between any group that is discriminated against and the African American experience. This is where the frequent similarities are established between gay Americans and African Americans.

Similarities between gay American and African American social movement over the past four decades

Both African Americans and GLBT Americans had major physical battles that were turning points in their movements. One took place in Selma and the other at Stonewall. Each of these events were played out in the media and brought a massive level of national exposure to their causes. Both groups had prominent political/social leaders who were assassinated. Both groups have been the victims of hate crimes and other egregious acts of violence against them. Both groups are ultimately seeking to change and challenge the ideas and beliefs of the American culture in regards to their groups. Both groups' battles are just as much philosophical and idealistic as they are legal and political. Both used the tactics of protest and demonstrations, both saw internal shifts in attitudes from passivity in the earlier stages toward a more active and aggressive front, and both would eventually wage their battles in the arena of government and politics in terms of seeking equality.

Various organizations that have worked in conjunction with African Americans and GLBT Americans have identified these similarities. The National Organization of Women has equated racism, sexism, and homophobia as ultimately the same battle in America.[13] The Mattachine Society held as one of its guiding principles to "educate homosexuals and heterosexuals toward an ethical homosexual culture paralleling the cultures of the Negro, Mexican, and Jewish people."[14] The *Advocate Magazine*, one of the largest GLBT publications, said that comparisons between both groups are based upon gays being "the most socially acceptable targets" of hatred as Blacks once were.[15] The Congressional Black Caucus and the NAACP as organizations have officially been passive on this issue. However, in 2009 the chair of the NAACP at the time, Julian Bond, argued in a testimony before the New Jersey State Senate that "gay rights equal civil rights" and that "sexual disposition parallels race."[16] The late Coretta Scott King, wife of Dr. Martin Luther King, was an outspoken advocate for GLBT rights over the last few decades of her life; and there are some who argue that the GLBT American and African American causes and identity are relatively the same.

In light of these apparent similarities, there are three issues that are worthy of consideration in analyzing comparisons between GLBT Americans and African Americans. The first issue is nature (race and orientation), the second issue is the expression of that orientation (the role of sex and sexual liberation), and finally the role of faith, which in many respects becomes the controlling issue.

Gay American/African American Orientation: Is Homosexuality a Product of Nature?

If there were a universal and conclusive answer to this question that everyone could agree on, then there would be no homosexuality debate in America or in churches today. If homosexuality was indeed a natural proclivity that was not in any way affected by personal decisions, life experiences, exposure, any form of direct or indirect nurturing, or any other non-external factors, then a homosexual orientation would be equitable to ethnicity. If so, God's will on the subject would be clear and anything short of complete and total acceptance of this lifestyle and all practices and ideas associated with it by the church, government, and all public and private sectors would be contrary to the spirit of the Constitution and the Bible.

However, on this issue science is split and there is no biblical precedence for a homosexual orientation (we deal with this in greater detail below). This issue lends itself to psychological, spiritual, and scientific issues that would take volumes of research to properly address; and science and religion may come to different conclusions. In one sense, the question comes down to what to do when science and Scripture disagree and how does one resolve it. Science constantly evolves, while more orthodox views on faith tend to remain the same. One has to wonder what the relationship is between popular culture, which also evolves, and the integrity of scientific truth. This issue comes into play when looking at science's defense of homosexuality through the American Psychological and American Psychiatric Association.

In 1973 the American Psychiatric Association officially removed homosexuality from its list of *Diagnostic and Statistical Manual of Mental Disorders* (DSM). The DSM is the leading source by most in the health field in determining mental status. This determination took

QUESTION 4: Homosexuality in America:
Is African American Synonymous with Gay American?

87

place four years after the Stonewall riots and during the growing gay liberation movement. It has been argued that this decision was strongly influenced by internal politics stemming from the growing attitudes in the country as opposed to this being a purely science driven decision.[17] The American Psychological Association (APA) changed their policies in 1975 and acknowledged that public sentiment had some impact on the American Psychiatric Association's decision.[18]

Public sentiment also has had some impact on how sexual orientation changes or reparative therapy are viewed in the scientific community.

Sexual Orientation Changes

When individuals who have lived a public heterosexual lifestyle begin to embrace a homosexual lifestyle, this transition is commonly referred to as "coming out." This is seen as a liberating experience in embracing one's identity or in coming to peace with who a person is. The APA encourages coming out as an important step in psychological development and in coming to peace with one's identity.[19] However, on the issue of transitioning from homosexuality to heterosexuality, the APA has treated this process with more caution and reservation, as indicated in their 2009 study, "Appropriate Therapeutic Responses to Sexual Orientation." Here the APA encourages therapists to help their clients "cope with social prejudices against homosexuality." The APA is very skeptical of therapy and processes that seek to change or address changes in orientation.[20]

However, there are many organizations such as Exodus International in Florida who work with churches and other counseling ministries around the country and have been very successful in recovery efforts that help individuals who desire to change their orientation and sexual habits. The American Psychological Association cautions against such sexual orientation change efforts (SOCE) for the following reasons: such treatments do not always maintain sustained results, many of the treatments were biased and offered by organizations who had a predisposition against homosexuality as an orientation, and such treatments could cause harm on the grounds that some experienced a loss of sexual desire, depression, and even suicidal thoughts.[21]

This apprehension toward transitions from homosexuality to heterosexuality would appear to be indicative of some public sentiment on the issue, with many opposing any opinion or idea that would present opposing viewpoints on homosexuality, regardless of their basis or clear examples of how this form of counseling works. It can be argued that attacks on SOCE are not purely academic in nature, but also revolve around public opinion.

The issue of orientation and choosing is indeed a legitimate one, there is not much of a case that needs to be made about genetics being associated with race, but the door is wide open on sexual orientation. Despite these differences, the common belief is that regardless of one's orientation or ethnicity, there are certain human and civil rights that should be available to everyone. However, the distinctions between GLBT Americans and African Americans also exist on issues surrounding the expression of homosexuality, which is a sex act.

Gay Americans/African Americans: The Issue of Sex

The second challenge in establishing similarities between GLBT Americans and African Americans is surrounding the issue of the actual sex act. The GLBT American agenda is not just about homosexuals as people entitled to human and civil rights. It also involves, more broadly, the perpetuation of the idea that sex between people of the same gender is the same as heterosexual sex and that society should validate this non-restrictive sexual liberation and redefine what is acceptable sexual intimate behavior. The GLBT American revolution and agenda is in many respects just as much a sexual revolution as it is a human rights or civil rights revolution in terms of changing ideas in the American culture about sex.

In doing research and analysis in this subject, I have read several publications; watched a series of documentaries, lectures, and movies; and talked to many homosexuals to attempt to get a better understanding of the GLBT lifestyle and what their aims were and are. One of the overarching themes of the GLBT community is the acceptance of a more liberated sex life and an adjustment of what society deems as appropriate sexual behavior.[22] More recently, there have been children's books written that have been used in public schools with images of same-sex couples kissing to show the normalcy of this practice. There have been school districts that allow gay couples to go to the prom and cross-dressing in high school. There are churches that sanction sexual intercourse outside of marriage for homosexuals and heterosexuals.[23] In addition, what I discovered historically was the normalcy and frequency of a wide variety of multiple sex partners and orgies between adults.[24] Through much of

QUESTION 4: Homosexuality in America:
Is African American Synonymous with Gay American?

89

the literature and documentaries, there was frequent discussions of gay bathhouses, frequent sex parties in the backs of trucks, sex retreats, prostitution at bars, "one-night stands," etc.[25] While this sexual appetite may not be common to all GLBT people, these practices were not frowned upon nor viewed as infrequent occurrences that were only taken by a small radical sect of the community. These actions illustrated the lifestyle and transformation of this community.[26]

By no means am I implying that there has not been excessive sexually lascivious behavior in the African American community, or any other community for that matter, but the question comes down to what sexually lascivious behavior is. Redefining sex is central to the gay agenda. Should marriage be a precondition for sex? Is a committed monogamous relationship the same as marriage? Is sex and acts of affection between two people of the same sex the same as heterosexual relationships? Should all sexual relationships be monogamous? Should sodomy be illegal? Is casual sex acceptable? The act of sex is central to homosexuality in defining their cause.

☛ **Point of Reflection:**

What role should the government play in sex-related issues?

The first reaction that many may have is this: should the government be in the business of legislating what happens in the bedroom? While most on the Left and Right would probably say that the government should stay out of people's private sex lives; Liberals on the Left would say that homosexual practices are a civil liberty, and libertarians on the Right would echo that concern in championing individual rights and limited government, whether in the bank account or bedroom.

However, some will couple their belief of the government staying out of private sex decisions with the belief that the federal government should be very active in addressing the consequences of private sex decisions. If there is an expectation that the government be involved in the abortion debate in terms of expanding it, curtailing it, eliminating it, or funding it, then the government is involved on the back end of private sex decisions. If there is an expectation that the government is involved with sexually transmitted diseases (STDs) in terms of educating on how to avoid them, treating people who have been infected by them, or funding scientific research to find cures for them, then again the government is involved on the back end of private sex decisions. If the government is involved on the back end of private sex decisions, how much should the government be involved on the front end? Should the government get out of the front end and back end of private sex decisions? And why are churches so quiet on this issue?

This is clearly a values-based decision. Historically for African Americans, values-based decisions were primarily controlled by biblical standards and what the church deemed as appropriate behavior. For GLBT Americans, the role of the church has not been as large a factor in terms of shaping their cultural and social concerns. This is the third major distinction I see between GLBT Americans and African Americans: the role of faith in shaping their social movement and pattern of beliefs.

Gay American/African Americans: What Impact Does Faith Have in the African American and Gay American Community?

In many ways the similarities and differences between the two can best be understood in terms of the role of faith. Faith was and is the lifeline in the African American community. As discussed in Chapter 1, faith among many African Americans has primarily been expressed in adherence to the Bible, regular attendance and participation in a local congregation, and using the Bible as the ultimate authority and indicator of right and wrong. Everybody, regardless of their race, religion, or philosophy, has something that dictates to them right or wrong. For many it has been the Bible.

It would be nearly impossible to do any historical or cultural analysis of African Americans without seeing the overarching role of faith in the development of ideas and beliefs and in the development and organization of the freedom struggle. The church is arguably the single most important and vital institution in terms of the history and freedom struggle of African Americans. In analyzing GLBT Americans, there was and is an element of faith in defining their agenda, and there is a significant contingency of GLBT Americans who would identify themselves with a particular faith in terms of beliefs.[27] However, studies have found that there is a significant gap between identification and attitudes on faith between gay and straight Americans.[28] While faith is important in the GLBT community, it has not been as central to the GLBT agenda in defining their issues, organizing their events, and providing the motivating force in their quest for full acceptance. A good case study is the parallel between Selma and Stonewall, the two major turning points in history for both groups.

The Role of Faith: Selma and Stonewall

While the symbolism and historical impact of the events were the same, the content was extremely different. Selma was a protest organized by local pastors, as well as religious and community leaders. This protest began in a church on a Sunday afternoon after a church service to fight for voting rights. The Stonewall riots occurred in a mafia-owned bar in New York City and involved sex, drugs, illegal alcohol, prostitution, and police bribery.

The vast majority of leaders in the African American community were and are preachers who used their pulpits as a platform in organizing the community and the Bible as a basis for outlining morality and rationales for full inclusion of African Americans. While there are some GLBT leaders who identify themselves as religious leaders, the majority of the leaders in the GLBT movement, both past and present, such as Harry Hay, Harvey Milk, Barbara Gittings, Barney Frank, and Rita Mae Brown, did not come from the pulpit, nor is the Bible used with the same degree of authority or absolutism in outlining their agenda (we'll get into this further later in the chapter). One of the reasons that Christianity may not play such a large factor in the GLBT community may be due to the clear and overt passages that are in Scripture regarding homosexuality. Reconciling homosexuality with Christianity is a difficult task biblically.

The faith element was and is central to the African American experience. You would not have a slave rebellion, Underground Railroad, Freedmen's Bureau, Historically Black Colleges and Universities, Civil Rights Movement, or Black elected officials without an active church or faith element. While there have been some leaders and voices in the African American community who have distanced themselves from faith or involvement in church, for the most part the African American experience is a Christian experience. It is the internal role of faith in the African American community that I believe draws the greatest distinctions between both groups.

☛ **Point of Reflection:**

What does the Bible have to say about homosexuality?

When it comes to the Bible and homosexuality and the subsequent impact of the two on society, there really are three separate questions that need to be dealt with in the following order:

1. Does the Bible validate homosexuality?

2. Do I agree with the Bible's opinion on homosexuality?

3. How should the church or government respond to homosexuality?

More often than not, there is a tendency to merge these three questions. In merging the three, there is a tendency to make the Bible validate everything that is socially and culturally acceptable or there is a tendency to allow our opinion of what is socially and culturally acceptable to become intermingled with a biblical position. Our opinion of homosexuality really should not have any bearing on what the Bible has to say about the subject. In some sense the issue of homosexuality as it relates to the Bible is a matter of biblical interpretation as discussed in Chapter 1.[29]

There are six common references in the Bible that deal directly and explicitly with the act of same-sex sexual relationships:

Genesis 19:1–9 and Judges 19:22–25

The verse in Genesis tells the story of a man named Lot who lived in the city of Sodom. Lot had two male angelic figures come to visit his home. The men in the town tried very aggressively to get Lot to bring the visitors outside the home so that the men of the city could have sex (rape) these two men. Lot offered the men of the city his two virgin daughters for sex as opposed to letting the men have access to the visitors. The men did not want the daughters. The men of the city continued to try to aggressively get into Lot's house to rape the two visitors. The visitors pulled Lot back into the house and smote all of the men of the city with blindness. God eventually destroyed the entire town of Sodom with the exception of Lot's family.

A similar situation happened in the Book of Judges, with vile living, abuse, potential rape, and homosexuality. Many will point out that the story in Sodom was not exclusively about homosexuality, which is correct; however homosexuality was a major component of it.

> Though shalt not lie with mankind, as with womankind: it is abomination.
>
> —LEVITICUS 18:22

If a man also lie with mankind, as he lieth with a woman, both of them have committed an abomination: they shall surely be put to death; their blood shall be upon them.

—LEVITICUS 20:13

Wherefore God also gave them up to uncleanness through the lust of their own hearts, to dishonor their own bodies between themselves: Who changed the truth of God into a lie, and worshipped and served the creature more than the Creator, who is blessed forever. Amen. For this cause God gave them up to vile affections: for even their women did change the natural use into that which is against nature: And likewise also the men, leaving the natural use of the woman, burned in their lust one toward another; men with men working that which is unseemly, and receiving in themselves that recompense of their error which was meet.

—ROMANS 1:24–27

Know ye not that the unrighteous shall not inherit the kingdom of God? Be not deceived: neither fornicators, nor idolaters, nor adulterers, nor effeminate, nor abusers of themselves with mankind, nor thieves, nor covetous, nor drunkards, nor revilers, nor extortioners, shall inherit the kingdom of God.

—1 CORINTHIANS 6:9–10

From reading these passages that deal directly with the subject of homosexuality, it would appear obvious that the Bible does not in any way endorse the practice of sexual relationships between people of the same sex. There are no passages in the Bible that deal directly with homosexuality that view it positively or are indifferent toward it. The Bible was written by several different authors, during different dispensations (economies, administrations or sets of rules), and during various historical time periods; the message seems to be universal regarding this practice. This is the position taken by many Christians. *These passages do not spread a message of hate nor do they degrade people.* Rather these passages take a clear position on the issue of sexual relationships between people of the same sex.

Theologians on the Left and Right agree with the direct messages from these passages; however, theologians on the Left will invalidate the authenticity of these texts and/or adjust the meaning of the scriptures based upon their methods of interpretation in order to establish biblical support for homosexuality. Liberal theologians argue that the passages in the Old Testament were time limited and intended for a certain audience or did not focus on homosexuality as a sin.[30] The story of Sodom was seen more so as condemning rape, sexual aggression, and coercions as opposed to homosexual behavior, in their view.[31] The New Testament passages in 1 Corinthians, according to Liberal Theologians, are seen to be also geared toward the original audiences who allegedly delved into male prostitution and having sex with minors, so the condemnation was against illicit sex as opposed to consensual or loving sex between adults. More generally, they'll often assert that God is a God of love, so He does not have a problem with two people who are in a monogamous, loving relationship whether heterosexual or homosexual. The Romans text, again according to Liberal Theologians, was allegedly rooted in Paul's culture at the time and the lack of understanding of a sexual orientation, which is absent from Scripture; so heterosexuals having sex with homosexuals was going against their natural orientation or purpose which was similar to idol worship.[32]

At best, this level of adjustment and interpretation would render extremely vague inferences of approval of homosexuality; but nothing explicit, clear, or direct from Scripture. Some theologians will take the position that the guest facilitator did that I spoke about from my time in college: drawing parallels between what the Bible has to say about homosexuality and what the Bible has to say about other issues such as the role of women, seafood, and slavery to attempt to illustrate an alleged parallel of outdated and nonpractical scriptures.[33] But the guidelines in condemnation of homosexuality are clear, direct, and exact. They occur both in the Old and New Testament; and there are no scriptures that celebrate or view homosexuality in a positive light.[34] In the case of women, we have many biblical examples of women who were celebrated.[35] We also find women in leadership positions such as Deborah and Mary Magdalene. The Bible also goes as far as telling husbands to love their wives as Christ has loved the church, so there is a celebration of women in Scripture. In the case of slavery, as theologian Robert Gagnon points out, there is no mandate for slavery.[36] It is not mentioned during the pre-Fall period, and the story of Israel suggests a positive view of the liberation of slavery.[37] We just do not find these same variations and validations when it comes to homosexuality. The weight of finding clear biblical validation for homosexuality is difficult at best.

This massive manipulation of Scripture on the Left, along with bringing in personal experiences and beliefs and treating other historical documents with more authority in validating truth in Scripture is the only

QUESTION 4: Homosexuality in America:
Is African American Synonymous with Gay American?

95

way to make homosexuality biblically valid. If such an undertaking is necessary to establish a line of thought, then one has to question whether we approach Scripture to seek truth or whether we approach Scripture to create and validate truth. A good litmus test is this: is there anything in Scripture that one could fundamentally disagree with, yet can still accept as being true or valid? Or is it that we seek to adjust the meaning of Scripture whenever there is disagreement with Scripture in order to make Scripture fit our lives and to fit perfectly into what we deem as a just culture? It is for this reason that I believe it is necessary to separate the three questions mentioned above, beginning with the inquiry into what the Bible has to say, absent any of our personal beliefs. Once a determination has been made about what the Bible has to say, then the determination should be made about personal opinion and the role of the Bible in our society.

Christianity in its purest sense is about love and unity for all people. Christianity involves the balance of love with standards, which means God's standards do not compromise His love for each person and His love for each person does not change His standards. These two competing factors have made compromise in the church a very difficult issue. Compromise from a biblical perspective would then have to involve a healthy blend of love, compassion, *and* standards.

☞ **Point of Reflection:**

Is there a middle ground on the issue in the church?

In the heat of the discussion, there is a view that has been overlooked of late. This is the idea that it is possible to disagree with the practice of homosexuality without expressing hate or discrimination toward individuals. The dichotomy of disapproving of a practice yet not allowing that to affect friendship is the posture taken by many Christians and is the example of Jesus.

We have the case of Jesus when He caught the woman in adultery. At no point in the story did Jesus sanction or change His belief about her sexually lascivious behavior. However, His compassion for her as a person was evident, and He did not allow His great disdain for her actions to affect His relationship or compassion for her as a person. Nor did He allow His concern for her as a person and His desire to protect her in the face of her accusers to change His opinion about her actions.

(See John 8:1–11.) This is the posture of Jesus in separating the actions from the actors.

Unfortunately, there are some who have not understood this balance and have allowed their love and compassion for people to filter into complete disdain and discarding of Scripture. This is due to a lack of understanding that compassion and conviction are not enemies and can coexist. And there are others who have allowed their frustration and disagreement with the practice of homosexuality to filter into negative attitudes of hate, bigotry, and acts of violence toward homosexuals, which does not express by any means the message of the Bible.

The lack of understanding of the different tiers of those who express dissent for homosexuality has led to the use of terms and labels that are ambiguous and can be construed as derogatory and slanderous. Single terms with a multiplicity of meanings used to describe large groups of people in any venue have the tendency to do more harm than good. Such is the case with the term homophobic or homophobia.

☛ **Point of Reflection:**

Homophobia/Homophobic: What do(es) the word(s) really mean?

The origins of the term *homophobia* go back to George Weinberg's book *Society and the Healthy Homosexual* and a 1971 article written by Kenneth Shaw, "Homophobia: A Tentative Personality Profile."[38] Going back again to the historical context of both pieces of literature, each was written around the same time as the gay and lesbian liberation movement during the late '60s and early '70s where attitudes and opinions in the American culture were changing.

The idea of phobia expresses "fear of" in terms of a psychological disorder or in trepidation, very rarely if ever is the suffix attached to a word in the context of a sound or informed scholarly or biblical disagreement. In the context of dissent for homosexuality, such a label leads one to believe that disagreement is not coupled with respect. The strongest advocates for the biblical validation of homosexuality even have to agree that there is overwhelming evidence given to the opposite perspective that the Bible does not approve of this practice. In acknowledging this fact, there is massive literature and scholarship that is aimed toward establishing a biblical precedent for homosexuality. If the evidence in Scripture were not as direct and candid, then this volume of literature to establish a precedent would not be necessary. So is a sound disagreement worthy of label?

Homophobia is not a positive or merely descriptive term but frequently is used as a derogatory label for those who express dissent with the practice of homosexuality. The term *homophobia* does not allow for a humble and respectful disagreement but seems to be levied at any form of disagreement. It really only lends itself to hate and bigotry. If disagreements on the subject came down to a matter of interpretation or understanding of the Bible and has nothing to do with hate, fear, or arrogance, then overarching broad terms such as *homophobia* or labeling someone as homophobic is damaging in trying to bring peace and civility to a very challenging issue in our culture.

Even in the abortion debate, the terms *pro-choice* and *pro-life* represent two competing and practically polar opposite viewpoints. These terms still carry a degree of civility that expresses a reasoned or informed difference of opinion, even though the differences in opinions are strong. So then in the spirit of bringing civility to a very contentious issue, the question remains of how to proceed on this issue, with such strong opinions that exist regarding homosexuality in America.

☛ **Point of Reflection:**

How then does the church and government proceed on this issue?

So then:

1. To some homosexuality is a matter of civil and human rights.

2. To some homosexuality is part of a larger agenda to redefine the family structure and reshape attitudes and opinions about sex and sexuality.

3. To some homosexuality is a product of nurture.

4. To some it is a product of nature.

5. To some homosexuality is a deviant behavior.

6. To some it is a different behavior.

7. To some homosexuality is a matter of private sex decisions.

8. To some homosexuality is a public issue.

9. To some the government should completely stay out of the issue in terms of legislating practices associated with it, making special provisions for homosexuals, or financially supporting actions to remedy the consequences of private sex decisions.

10. To some homosexuals can be separated from homosexuality.

11. To some the two are forever connected.

12. To some the Constitution is the authority on the issue.

13. To some the Bible is the authority on the issue.

14. To some this is a significant issue that deserves attention by the government and church.

15. To others this issue is not that important.

Looking through the lenses of faith and race in analyzing the issues above, there would appear to be three practical vantage points in addressing homosexuality.[39]

- **Position 1:** Disagreeing with the practice (homosexuality) and having a great disdain for the people (homosexuals)

- **Position 2:** Disagreeing with practice (homosexuality) and yet fully embracing the people (homosexuals)

- **Position 3:** Full agreement with the practice and fully embracing the people

While these three positions may not represent the totality of perspectives on homosexuality, they do for the most part represent the general frameworks to which the church and government have chosen to address this issue.

Position 1 and Position 3 both represent the more popular viewpoints on this issue in that these perspectives are the ones that normally get aired on cable news networks and have for the most part set the tenor of the debate. However, Position 2 is rarely ever voiced or explored because it lacks the passion and sometimes anger that is associated between those who advocate Positions 1 and 3. Position 2 may be where many people can peaceably balance their admiration for all people, their respect and deference for Scripture, equality of basic human and civil rights, and their desire to have a peaceful society.

In the church world, Position 2 is the only position that the Bible advocates in terms of dealing with any behavior that would not be sanctioned in Scripture, whether adultery, drunkenness, lying, or anything else. In government, Position 2 has been the main vantage point through which this issue has been addressed. This is how gay marriage has constantly been challenged, yet hate crimes laws and employment discrimination laws for gays and lesbians have been accepted. But, as we are continuing to see, the passion associated with Positions 1 and 3 is drowning out the voice of Position 2.

As I analyze the major components of this issue, taking into account the love for people, the love for Scripture, and the desire for a peaceful society, my first observation when analyzing candidates is not at the specific policies that a candidate offers on this issue. Rather, I attempt to see from which vantage point they approach the issue of homosexuality in America.

Question 5

ABORTION: WHO LEFT THE GATE OPEN?
AND SHOULD WE WORK TO CLOSE IT
OR SHOULD WE OPEN IT WIDER?

A Case Study on the Reality of Abortion in America: Kermit Gosnell and the Women's Medical Society[1]

ON FEBRUARY 18, 2010, the Federal Bureau of Investigation, along with detectives from the Philadelphia District Attorney's office and representatives from the Pennsylvania Departments of State and Health, conducted a raid of the Women's Medical Society, a clinic in Philadelphia, based upon an ongoing investigation of illegal prescription drug activity.

What the investigators discovered upon entering this facility, which was located in a low-income African American community, was a functioning clinic with blood stains everywhere. The building reeked of cat urine with flea-infested cats roaming around the office. The investigators observed non-working medical equipment. Overall, the office was considered unsanitary. In this facility, many women were treated in ways that violated the laws and some received life-altering injuries. Two women died due to failed procedures at the clinic, and many *fully delivered*, living, and breathing babies were murdered on a regular basis for over four decades, with their severed body parts stored in freezers, jars, and trash bags.

At this facility procedures were performed with used and reused unsanitary medical instruments which spread STDs between patients. This facility, which was also one of the largest Oxycontin providers in the state, illegally prescribed and administered prescription drugs and sedatives during medical procedures at any level that the patients requested and could afford. All of these actions were performed under the facade of an abortion clinic.

This multimillion dollar enterprise was run by Dr. Kermit Gosnell, an African American physician who enjoyed taking pictures of his patients' genitals on his cell phone for no obvious medical reason and who was not trained or certified in obstetrics or gynecology. Yet, for over four decades he ran this state-certified abortion clinic where he performed thousands of abortions illegally for patients from all around the country, at all stages of pregnancy, including the twenty-ninth and thirtieth weeks. Dr. Gosnell ran this criminal enterprise with the assistance of several unlicensed and unqualified workers, including a high school student and two unlicensed medical school graduates who presented themselves to the community as doctors. The most traumatizing fact about this entire story was not just the heinous acts of evil going on inside this clinic, but the gross indifference and cover-up by government agencies on state and local levels, as well as a network of abortion organizations, fellow doctors, and some in the community.

According to the findings of the Grand Jury that was convened after the raid, the State Department of Health adopted unofficial polices, where abortion clinics across the state were not regularly monitored or inspected. This practice was primarily due to the "policy preferences" of state leaders. The Grand Jury found that "the State Department of Health inexplicably allows abortion clinics, *alone*, to go unmonitored." The Grand Jury report revealed that nail salons in the state were more closely monitored than abortion clinics. Testimony to the Grand Jury revealed that there was a meeting in 1999 with "high-level government officials" where the decision was made to relax inspections of abortion clinics with the understanding that more inspections would possibly reveal several clinics not in compliance; so a hands-off approach was adopted.

Prior to the raid in 2010, the State Department of Health had not conducted an inspection of this clinic since 1993, although certifications last for only a year. The clinic initially received state certification in 1979, yet the raid in 2010 revealed that many of the findings of the initial certification were inaccurate. The next documented review was in 1989—ten years later. At this review the state found the clinic in violation of several major abortion statutes; yet the clinic received its approval for another year. The following two reviews occurred in 1992 and 1993 with the state finding some of the same violations; but the clinic continued to receive its certification. Over the next sixteen years the state received several complaints/inquiries about the clinic from attorneys, pediatricians, a public medical examiner who concluded that a baby was stillborn after the mother received treatment at the clinic. In each instance, the state did not open an investigation. Unfortunately, they were not alone in their neglect.

There were several doctors who treated women at local hospitals due to complications from abortions performed by Dr. Gosnell. Many of these doctors failed to report their findings to the State Department of Health, although they were required to do so by law. The local government also failed to investigate several complaints that they had received in regards to the storage of aborted fetuses at the clinic.

The National Abortion Federation (NAF), an association of abortion providers, did a visit to the clinic, based upon Dr. Gosnell's request for admission to their association. At the visit the NAF discovered many of the illegal practices going on and denied the clinic admission to their organization, which was rare, but failed to report what was going on to the proper state and local authorities.

This case study reveals how wide the gates of abortion have opened in America and the extent to which many organizations and institutions will go in protecting abortion rights. How can so many people and organizations, without having any communication or planning among each other, all come to the same fundamental conclusion of keeping these evil practices quiet in hopes of protecting abortion rights?[2] This story gives the clearest example of the gross indifference in our society toward abortion and toward the actual people involved in the process. The questions become: How did we come to a place where the gates of abortion have swung open so widely? Where should we as a nation go from here? Many of the issues surrounding abortion in America are seen in the facts surrounding the life of a young mother and a baby in the early '70s.

The Roots of the Modern Abortion Debate in America

Norma Jean McCorvey (the Young Mother)

Norma Jean McCorvey was born in 1947 in Louisiana and at a young age relocated with her family to Texas. Norma's very challenging childhood was characterized by regular physical and verbal abuse by her mother, incarceration in juvenile detention centers, being raped by adult males and females[3] and being involved in homosexual practices[4] at a very young age, and running away from home. During Norma's teen years she dropped out of high school, got married, became pregnant, and was physically abused.[5] During her first pregnancy she was physically abused by her husband and began developing gay and lesbian relationships. After leaving her husband and spending much of her life in poverty, her abusive mother got custody of Norma's child.[6] Norma began both using and selling drugs.[7] She also had serious emotional challenges and suffered through depression before becoming pregnant for a second time.[8]

Norma gave up her second child for adoption immediately after the child was born.[9] When Norma got pregnant a third time at the age of twenty-one, she decided that she did not want to go forward with the pregnancy. She felt like her life was not in a place to handle a child, and she considered herself a "deadbeat, a bum, a twenty-one-year-old nobody at the end of [her] rope."[10] She did not want to have this baby. Her former gynecologist told her about the abortion process, which was illegal at the time, and that he could not help her get one.[11] She eventually met with two young lawyers who were trying to overturn the Texas statute that made abortion illegal.[12] The attorneys needed someone who was pregnant for their case, while Norma's focus was getting rid of the baby.[13] In hopes of getting an abortion, Norma lied and told the attorneys that she was raped thinking that this would give her a stronger opportunity to secure an abortion.[14] Norma agreed to sign on and be a part of their case under the pseudonym *Jane Roe*.[15]

During this third pregnancy Norma continued to abuse drugs and alcohol[16] and also tried to kill herself.[17] Although Norma was the plaintiff in the case, she was never present at any of the hearings nor did she have contact with the attorneys during the trial.[18] She felt that she was just a pawn in their game, nothing but a "piece of paper."[19]

Although the case was about abortion, Norma never had an abortion and eventually gave birth to the baby and put the child up for adoption. Although the attorneys would ultimately be successful in their attempt to overturn abortion laws, after having this third baby, Norma had several unsuccessful suicide attempts[20] and didn't talk to the attorneys until a year after the baby was born, the case proceeded without her.[21]

The Baby That Got It All Started

Born in 1970 in the State of Texas to a mother of Cherokee and Cajun decent named Norma McCorvey who did not believe that she was ready to take on the responsibility of a baby, McCorvey's baby was given up for adoption immediately after her birth and has lived in virtual obscurity ever since. We have little to no information about her biological father, we know the child has at least two older biological sisters the oldest named Melissa born in 1965 and her second eldest sibling also given up for adoption a few years prior to her birth. The obscurity surrounding this child's life began from the moment that the baby was conceived, with many people arguing that this baby should have never been born. Although we know little about this child who today is in her forties, we do know for certain that this is indeed a person who does exist, and this person is in many ways a tangible representative of the state of abortion in America.

Who/What left the Gate Open on Abortion: Numbness to Abortion in America?

> I was not really scared. I was not really depressed, either. I was down too low to feel the pain or shame that was stored up inside me. In other words, I was outside the range of normal human feeling. Past really caring. Numb.[22]

These words were the sentiments of Norma McCorvey after discovering she was pregnant for the third time. In many ways these words reflect the American sentiment toward abortion. We as a nation have become so indifferent and comfortable with pregnancies ending in abortion that many have lost all feelings toward abortion; terminating babies has become so normal in our country that many do not recognize, or in worst cases, do not care how big this practice has grown.

- Since 1973 there have been over 50 million abortions in America.[23]

- On average since 1973, over 1 million abortions are performed annually.[24]

- One in three American women will have an abortion before she reaches the age of forty-five.[25]

- Half of the pregnancies among Americans are unintended; four out of ten of these unintended pregnancies end in abortion.[26]

- In 2008, 19 percent of all pregnancies ended in abortion; on average it has been around 20 percent since 1973.[27]

- 36.4 percent of all abortions in 2006 were performed on African American mothers, who only make up 12 percent of the population.[28]

Fifty million abortions, with one million added annually, ultimately make up an entire generation or culture that never existed, and the number continues to grow at a very rapid pace. A good indicator of assessing one's attitudes on abortion is how you respond to the 50 million: Is it a cause of celebration? Is it a cause of shame and hurt? or Is there indifference and apathy toward it?

Who/What Left the Gate Open on Abortion: Unmandated Reporting Process?

☞ **Points of Reflection:**

How many abortions take place annually?

Why is there such a mystery?

While 50 million is a large number in and of itself, the realty is there have been far more abortions performed in America; but the process of getting information on abortions is just as faulty and covert as the actual abortion process. There are two sources for getting national abortion data in the United States; one is the Center for Disease Control and Prevention (CDC), the only federal government source, and the other is the Alan Guttmacher Institute (AGI), which is a private organization and a subsidiary of Planned Parenthood.[29]

The CDC only reports data that they receive on a voluntary basis from some of the State Health Departments in its annual "Abortion Surveillance Report." As of 2011, only forty-six states mandated that abortion providers report statistics to their state. California, which is the largest state in the country, is one of the states that *does not* require that abortion data is reported. In each of the forty-six states that have abortion reporting mandates, there is no uniform process of collecting data or determining which data needs to be reported—such as when, how, and on whom the abortion was performed. None of the states are mandated to report their statistics to the CDC.[30] According to AGI, these variances from the reporting states have led to some states underreporting 40–50 percent of the abortions that actually take place.[31]

In the case of the Guttmacher Institute (AGI), they get their data from sending out direct surveys to all abortion providers in the country. This normally reveals a higher number than what is reported by the CDC, yet their figures are not always accurate because the reports are still voluntary.[32] In 2007, the CDC reported 827,609 abortions performed annually and the Guttmacher Institute reported roughly 1.2 million.

So, while 50 million is a large number, based upon the more accurate statistics from the AGI, the realty is there are more abortions taking place than what has been reported. This inconclusive reporting really causes one to wonder why the federal and state governments have not taken more control in providing more accurate data on such a high profile issue. How can a sound discussion even take place on the reality of abortion if we cannot determine what the true impact is?

The volume and frequency at which abortion takes place, along with the flawed underreporting of abortions, possibly provide some context to the dehumanization and desensitization of abortion. In others words, some may be apathetic and indifferent toward this lost generation because of how the abortion debate has been analyzed and framed.

☛ **Points of Reflection:**

Is abortion as serious as other issues?

Should abortion be a political deal breaker?

On a broader level, when the issue of abortion is seen as nothing but one in a series of women's rights issues, then it becomes equal with other women's rights issues such as "equal work for equal pay" or "voting rights." When a position on abortion is seen as nothing but a plank in a party's platform, then a pro or con position can easily be bargained away for any other issue that is politically expedient. We have seen both Democrats and Republicans engage in such bargaining on this issue.

The political Left has been pretty consistent in their support of women having a right to choose whether or not to have an abortion, which ultimately is an indicator of indifference toward the act of abortion. The political Left has been so dominated by abortion rights that it has been almost two decades since there has been a national figure on the political Left who was pro-life. The political Right has had both supporters and nonsupporters of abortion in major leadership positions in the party, which is also a sign of growing indifference toward abortion.

While many factors can be attributed to the overall dehumanization and growing in difference or the "open gate" on abortion, probably the greatest factor is a look into how the Supreme Court handled this issue in 1972 in making abortion a viable option during pregnancy.

Who/What Left the Gate Open on Abortion: The United States Supreme Court with Roe v Wade?

On January 22, 1973, the Supreme Court ruled in favor of Norma McCorvey in her argument that antiabortion laws in the State of Texas and around the country were unconstitutional on the grounds that the ninth and fourteenth Amendments of the Constitution implicitly instituted a right to privacy that includes the right of a mother to have an abortion.[33] The court also ruled that unborn babies are not protected or considered under the constitution as "persons," therefore they are not entitled to an absolute or unequivocal right to life.[34] The court continued that as the pregnancy develops, the state has some interest in protecting the life of the unborn baby.[35]

☛ **Point of Reflection:**

Activist Supreme Court judges: Did the judges overstep their responsibilities in the court decision or were they merely interpreting the law?

The court's ruling on the case was somewhat conflicting. The ruling stated that the right to an abortion was protected by the Constitution and unborn babies are not considered as persons, yet the state did have some interest during the pregnancy in protecting the life of the unborn fetus. So to resolve this dilemma which the court created, the court instituted principles and a litmus test into the case that neither the prosecution nor defense asked for.[36] The court decided to break down pregnancies into trimesters in determining when abortions were legal and when they were illegal.[37]

One of the many concerns with the court taking this action was that they went outside of their scope. State legislatures are intended to develop policies, and, in doing so, all public policies are subject to and controlled by public opinion or *"what the people want."* The idea of a Supreme Court justice creating standards as to when abortion should and should

QUESTION 5: Abortion: Who Left the Gate Open?
And Should We Work to Close It or Should We Open It Wider?

109

not be legal is arguably overstepping its bounds. Sarah Weddington, the attorney representing Norma McCorvey (Roe), was even surprised by this decision. She asked the court to rule on whether abortion was completely protected by the Constitution regardless of the stage.

What this decision ultimately did was two things:

1. Placed less value on unborn babies as a whole than they had prior to this decision

2. Instituted a principle that the decision of a mother whether or not to have a baby was given greater weight than the personhood of an unborn baby

This decision ultimately redefined family values in America, and in the decades that would follow it would go on to have a major impact in all of America, particularly in the African American community, which historically has not been as aggressive with this issue as with other issues.

☛ **Point of Reflection:**

Why the apparent silence in the African American community about abortion?

Most African American Christians do indeed contend that abortion is a moral issue and that the Bible does speak directly to this issue. The concern is that abortion is not regarded as the only moral issue. Unfortunately, what has happened is that some on the Right have championed abortion yet have remained silent on other important issues facing African Americans, which has caused some in the African American community to display their frustration in backing away from the abortion issue. In doing so, they have allowed their frustration to push abortion to the back burner because economic and/or racial issues have not been treated with the same level of importance by some in the Christian community. As a result, what, or more appropriately, who have suffered are the babies. This theory on the silence of abortion in the African American community is supported in the previously discussed "Dynamic of Shifting Theological Priorities (Ideologies)."[38]

This dynamic regarding abortion is illustrated in a recent PEW research poll where 58 percent of African Americans say abortion is morally wrong. Also, 40 percent of African Americans overall and 42 percent of African American Protestants say abortion should be illegal, which is a significant number in terms of dissent for this issue.[39] Yet

50 percent of African Americans and 42 percent of African American Protestants say that abortion is not a critical issue.[40] An even higher number of African Americans typically vote for pro-choice candidates in presidential elections.

So the idea that nearly half of African Americans oppose abortion and/or think that it is morally wrong, yet they do not carry this dissent to the polls, indicates that there must be other factors which superseded abortion and have led to the ultimate silence and passivity on this issue.

Who/What Left the Gate Open on Abortion: African American Abortion Apathy?

In understanding the apparent apathy in the Black community toward abortion, we must also return to another principle introduced in Question 2; the fact that there is a lack of a line-item veto in the electoral process (see Question 1), in voting for a candidate or party. Most times it is impossible to distinguish which individual issues one favors and which individual issues are disagreed with.

African American voting trends indicate that abortion for many African Americans is not a strong enough issue to supersede the issues that abortion has been packaged with. The pro-choice (support of abortion) position, which is most times championed by the Left, is frequently packaged with fiscal and racially progressive policies and rhetoric which many African Americans tend to support. In 2008, the Joint Center for Political and Economic Studies found that 62 percent of African Americans believed that the economy/poverty was the most important issue facing our country. This importance of poverty doubled from 2004 when only 31 percent of African Americans saw this as the most important issue.[41] In 2008, this study found that the second leading issue was a tie between healthcare, the war in Iraq, and other, with 7 percent of African Americans believing that these issues were most important.[42] In 2004 and 2008, abortion was not considered as one of the top three issues for African Americans. Therefore, with the pro-choice or affirmative abortion position being packaged with issues that African Americans find most important, there is a tendency to support candidates and parties who favor abortion, which on one level has helped to expand abortions.

In reverse, the pro-life position is frequently packaged with strict fiscal Conservatism, minimal entitlement spending on social programs besides Social Security, nonsupport for aggressive government intervention in healthcare (less healthcare regulation), and strong support for massive military spending. These themes have not always resonated with many African American voters. In a sense, abortion has become overshadowed by high military spending and less healthcare regulation. Arguably, many African Americans are not voting in favor of abortion rights, but rather they are voting against a passive government whose fiscal priorities seem to exclusively be concerned with national defense.

While this theory may offer some context as to why many African Americans have been silent on abortion, there are still some unanswered questions. Because so much of Black history has been rooted in protecting and valuing all life and fighting for full acceptance, one has to wonder why this theme has not manifested itself with abortion or how the preservation of life has not superseded other issues.

☛ **Point for Reflection:**

How does abortion fit into Black political and social history?

Most of the themes in Black political and cultural history have centered on justice, equality, peace, and the preservation of life. Whether we are talking about the Three-Fifths Compromise, the Underground Railroad, the Scottsboro Seven, The Little Rock Nine, the Tuskegee Experiment, Jim Crow, Emmitt Till, the Civil Rights Movement in the '60s, Black Power in the '70s, the Stop the Violence Movement in the '80s, or Rodney King in the '90s, there has always been a very high premium placed on protecting, preserving, and valuing all life and providing fundamental fairness for all people. But in the midst of these challenges, abortion, which is similar to the above stated issues in that it deals with the discarding and/or devaluing of life, has somewhat slipped through the cracks and is viewed as not being a part of the canon of experiences that have framed African American political and cultural history.

The political and cultural perspective of abortion, which has separated it from the scars of the past, is that abortion and abortion rights have been presented as an asset both culturally and politically to African Americans and have been championed from the pulpit by African American leaders.

Abortion framed exclusively as a Constitutional right and civil liberty

The argument is that abortion rights are a constitutional right, and taking away this right will somehow disadvantage African Americans.

In this view, "abortion rights" are seen as being more important than the actual act of "abortion" itself. Abortion rights are viewed as being similar to voting rights, freedom of speech, and integration, as opposed to abortion being seen as destroying a group of people and as a form of euthanasia, eugenics, and genocide. Protecting abortion rights for many has been framed in Black history as a fight for equal rights as opposed to a fight to preserve and protect life. Therefore, abortion has been packaged as a plea for justice and equality, which have been at the heart of African American political participation.

Abortion framed exclusively as an economic issue

In addition, Black political and cultural history has also had major themes of economic equality and personal responsibility. This is another tool that has been used in attempting to place abortion in the context of Black political history. Abortions have been framed as an economic asset to African Americans individually and at large. This was one of the main methods that was used in getting buy-in from African American leaders on this issue. This focus on economics and constitutional rights continues to cover up a very dark and malicious intent by some of the founders of the abortion movement in America.

Who/What Left the Gate Open on Abortion: Margaret Sanger and Her Hidden Use of Eugenics and Racism?

☛ **Point of Reflection:**

Fact or fiction: Genocide, eugenics, and racism are hidden in abortion rights?

> More children from the fit, less from the unfit...that is the chief issue of birth control.[43]
>
> —MARGARET SANGER

The birth control movement of the early twentieth century paved the way for the abortion movement of the mid to late twentieth century. It is impossible to do an analysis of the birth control movement without the focus being on Margaret Sanger, the lady who coined the term "birth control" and founded the American Birth Control League which would eventually change its name to Planned Parenthood of America, one of the largest abortion providers of today. It is impossible to do an analysis of Margaret Sanger's motives, actions, and methods without seeing very

dark, troubled, and ugly motives filled with eugenics, neo-Malthusianism
(a population control doctrine), and racism as part of her motivation.

Margaret Sanger was raised in Corning, New York, in the late nine-
teenth century, as the sixth of eleven children. She lived with both of
her parents in poverty. Margaret was strongly influenced by her father,
a devout socialist and atheist who abhorred the dogmas of religion and
was a follower of Robert Ingersoll.[44] Growing up in poverty, she repudi-
ated the size of her family based upon her belief that smaller families
were happier than larger families because they had more resources.[45]

In her adult years, she became a nurse and was very active in
socialist causes in New York City.[46] After spending some time in France
researching their family limitation laws,[47] she founded the National
Birth Control League in New York City, the first in the United States,
and she began to publish a radical magazine about women's health issues
and women's liberation causes.[48] Her magazine would be banned by the
United States Post Office under the Comstock Law, and she would be
charged in federal Court for its distribution. Before the trial ended, she
left the United States for Europe and continued study and research on
this issue.[49]

In Europe she was influenced by the teachings of Thomas Robert
Malthus, an economist, preacher, and contemporary of Adam Smith.[50]
Malthusianism was the belief that increased family sizes would have a
negative impact on the food supply and on the economy; more people
in the population would lead to lower wages in overcrowded manufac-
turing industries. His belief was that the population could and should be
controlled via late marriages and sexual abstinence until one was ready
for children.[51] Malthus did not support birth control and other forms of
contraception for religious reasons, and he was against government subsidies to the poor on the grounds that it encouraged poverty.[52] His stance
was that through this limited sexual reproduction by the poor and late
marriages, poverty could be addressed.[53]

Neo-Malthusianism believed in the same fundamental premise of overpopulation negatively impacting the economy as Malthusianism, but dif-
fered on the belief of sexual restraint being a reality. Neo-Malthusianism
advocated various forms of contraception to curtail overpopulation.[54]
This belief did not share the same religious dogmas on the subject as
Malthusianism.[55] Sanger came back to the United States strongly influenced by Neo-Malthusianism and argued that birth control would

eradicate poverty and through restricting population size all social evils would end.[56]

While it can be argued that women's liberation and poverty framed Sanger's passion for birth control, what arguably was her greatest motivation for birth control was eugenics, a cause which she championed in her life.

Eugenics, Birth Control, and Abortion Joined at the Hip!

Eugenics is "the study of all agencies under social control which can improve or impair the quality of future generations."[57] The term was coined by Sir Francis Galton, an anthropologist, statistician, and cousin of Charles Darwin, who studied trends in a variety of fields and among humans. Galton began to explore the ideas of hereditarianism, or the belief that the mental and psychological qualities of people were inherited.[58] Galton believed that any undesirable traits would outweigh desirable qualities, therefore he strongly abhorred reproduction between those with alleged good ("the fit") and those with alleged bad qualities (the "unfit").[59] In Galton's view, marriage should be regulated as well as assistance to the poor, in that it had the ability to encourage and sustain the unfit, which ultimately had a negative impact on the human race.[60] Galton advocated positive eugenics, which encouraged certain groups of people to continue to reproduce at a more rapid pace to improve and enhance the quality of the human race and to avoid what was known as race suicide, which was the practice of the alleged fit producing less, which threatened the quality of society.[61]

The belief in race suicide was a common part of American culture and was championed by U.S. presidents. Race suicide rejected birth control because it was sinful and also because the population needed to grow.[62] Race suicide was concerned that the lower class was expanding while the upper class was shrinking, which allegedly hurt the American culture.[63] This belief was rooted in Utopianism, which was alive in the United States and is the belief that it is possible to have a superior race.[64] While race suicide and positive eugenics sought to encourage certain groups to reproduce, negative eugenics sought to stunt certain groups from reproducing based upon the negative impact it would have on society.

Negative eugenics was rooted in practices that were aimed at curtailing the alleged "unfit" from reproducing. The "unfit" included immigrants, the disabled, the poor, and many minorities.[65] In America negative eugenics became a normal part of the American society, which was evident in 1927 when the Supreme Court, whose chief justice at the time was former President William Howard Taft, legalized compulsory sterilization in the Buck v. Bell case, a case which was organized by members of the eugenics movement.[66] This ruling led to over thirty states having sterilization laws on the books and over 60,000 people succumbing to mandatory sterilization. The headquarters for this eugenics operation was in Cold Springs Harbor, New York, where biologist Charles Davenport founded and operated the Eugenics Record Office (ERO).[67] The ERO wanted to stop reproduction from certain racial groups, those that were physically, medically, morally, culturally, and socially inadequate in the eyes of Davenport.[68]

For Davenport, the group of unfit included the feeble-minded, the pauper class, the inebriate class, criminals, epileptics, the insane, the constitutionally weak, the predisposed to specific diseases, the deformed, and the defective with certain organs (deaf, blind, mute), and their families.[69] Davenport's ideas were to wipe out the lower class and help create an alleged more perfect society and improve the quality of the human race. The primary tools for negative eugenics in America were sterilization and birth control.

During Margaret Sanger's quest for birth control, eugenics became one of, it not the ultimate motivation in advancing her crusade. In her 1922 book, *The Pivot of Civilization*, Sanger made it undoubtedly clear that her commitment and support for eugenics was the primary philosophy in advancing birth control. Sanger argued:

> There is but one practical and feasible program in handling the great problem of the feebleminded. That is, as the best authorities are agreed, to prevent the birth of those who would transmit imbecility to their descendant.[70]

Sanger went on to say, "Eugenics seems to me to be valuable in its critical and diagnostic aspects, in emphasizing the danger of irresponsible and uncontrolled fertility of the 'unfit' and feebleminded establishing a progressive unbalance in human society and lowering the birth rate among the 'fit.'"[71] In addition, in the *Birth Control Review*, a monthly magazine that Sanger began publishing in 1917, she argued, "Birth Control is not merely of Eugenic value but is practically identical…with the final aims of Eugenics."[72] Many of the articles in her *Birth Control*

Review celebrated eugenic values and ideas. In one article Sanger advocates sterilization:

> It now remains for the United States government to set a sensible example to the world by offering a bonus or a yearly pension to all obviously unfit parents who allow themselves to be sterilized by harmless and scientific means. In this way the moron and the diseased would have no posterity to inherit their unhappy condition. The number of feebleminded would decrease and a heavy burden would be lifted from the shoulders of the fit.[73]

Even more troubling with Sanger was her racist attitudes and her use of birth control to stifle reproduction among Blacks and poor people, who were considered by her and most eugenicists as part of the group of "unfit," "feebleminded," and "imbecile." Historian Linda Gordon argues that the birth control movement moved away from feminism and women's right's and began to focus on eugenics and the betterment of society.[74]

While some Sanger and birth control apologists will contend that Sanger was not a racist and that birth control was not meant to exterminate African Americans, there is too much weight to the contrary that makes her racial motives clear. Sanger was a friend of the Ku Klux Klan, and on several occasions she gave presentations at Klan rallies.[75] In 1921 when Sanger founded the American Birth Control League, she appointed as one of its directors Lothrop Stoddard, a Harvard graduate who was a historian, outspoken eugenicist, advisor to Adolf Hitler, and Klansman who had previously published *The Rising Tide of Color Against White World Supremacy*. In this study he argued that race, not politics, was the greatest factor in determining human affairs, and that the White race was superior to others and was the cause of most of the major triumphs in history.[76] Stoddard was very critical of all of the other major races in civilization besides Whites and particularly focused on Blacks. Stoddard argued:

> The Black race has never shown real constructive power. It has never built up a native civilization. Such progress as certain negro groups have made has been due to external pressure and has never long outlived that pressure's removal, for the negro, when left to himself, as in Haiti and Liberia, rapidly reverts to his ancestral ways. The negro is a facile, even eager, imitator; but there he stops. He adopts; but he does not adapt, assimilate, and give forth creatively again. The whole of history testifies to this truth. As the Englishman Meredith Townsend says: "None of the black races, whether negro or Australian,

QUESTION 5: Abortion: Who Left the Gate Open?
And Should We Work to Close It or Should We Open It Wider?

117

have shown within the historic time the capacity to develop civilization. They have never passed the boundaries of their own habitats as conquerors, and never exercised the smallest influence over peoples not black. They have never founded a stone city, have never built a ship, have never produced a literature, have never suggested a creed... There seems to be no reason for this except race.[77]

In addition, in 1917 Sanger began publication of the *Birth Control Review*, which had many articles that celebrated and showed the clear linkage between birth control and eugenics. The June 1925 issue of the *Birth Control Review* was almost exclusively dedicated to the linkage between birth control and eugenics.[78]

Margaret Sanger and the Negro Project

Sanger's racist motives were also seen in 1939 when she established the Negro Project as a program in the newly formed Birth Control Federation of America, which a few years later was renamed Planned Parenthood of America. On the surface, the theory behind the Negro Project was the same alleged theory behind most other eugenic programs in America: to allegedly assist the group of people, in this case Negros in the South, financially and culturally by giving them greater access to contraception to improve their plight in America and to control their fertility.[79]

Margaret Sanger recognized the clear and overt racial undertones of this program and decided to enlist the help of prominent African Americans in marketing the Negro Project in African American communities. To achieve this goal, Sanger turned to African American leaders such as W. E. Du Bois, Mary McLeod Bethune, and Adam Clayton Powell Jr. to assist in marketing and implementing this program in African American communities.[80] Sanger supporters argue that the appearance of prominent African Americans dispels any racist motives, but they fail to see the obvious: Sanger attempted to use African Americans as a front to hide her malicious intent. This was evident in the often quoted excerpt from a letter from Margaret Sanger to Clarence Gamble, which outlines her motives and use of African American leaders in promoting this "Negro Project":

> We do not want word to go out that we want to exterminate the negro population and the minister is the man who can straighten out that idea if it ever occurs to any of the more rebellious members.[81]

Unfortunately, there were many great African American leaders who bought into her eugenic ideals. However, their support for eugenics does not take away the racist intent. Unfortunately, there were some African American eugenicists who gave her ammunition which was frequently used to market this racist program in Black communities. The June 1932 issue of the *Birth Control Review* was almost exclusively targeted at African American issues related to eugenics and birth control. In an article in this issue, Du Bois stated:

> The mass of ignorant negroes still breed carelessly and disastrously, so that the increase among negroes, even more than the increase among whites, is far from that part of the population less intelligent and fit, and least able to rear their children properly.[82]

This use of African Americans as front people for the abortion/birth control/eugenics movement continued in the decades that followed. In 1966 the Planned Parenthood Federation of America awarded its first Margaret Sanger Awards to none other than Martin Luther King Jr. Almost a decade later, the organization appointed Faye Wattleton as its first African American president. Most Black elected officials today champion abortion, despite the fact that there is significant dissent against the issue in the Black community, as discussed earlier in this chapter. In many ways the aims of Margaret Sanger's covert racial agenda in her Negro Project has been and is continuing to be accepted today, with the proverbial gate being left open for abortion by African Americans. You can walk in nearly any predominantly African American community in the country and find several Planned Parenthood clinics.

Sanger also understood that there was a spiritual and faith-based component to the issue; so her plan, which was in many respects later adopted by the abortion movement, had to involve ministers in advocating birth control and abortion.

Who/What Left the Gate Open on Abortion: Preachers?

Preachers used as a tool in advancing abortion rights

☛ **Point of Reflection:**

What role, if any, should ministers play in supporting abortion rights in America?

> The minister's work is also important and he should be trained, per-
> haps by the Federation, as to our ideals and the goals that we hope
> to reach. We do not want word to go out that we want to extermi-
> nate the Negro population, and the minister is the man who can
> straighten out that idea if it ever occurs to any of their more rebel-
> lious members.[83]

Sanger understood the obvious power and influence of the pulpit in
the African American community. She understood that the pulpit in
the African American community was the proving ground for an idea.
Acceptance or rejection of any belief or idea for the most part had to
come via the pulpit. This may have been another concept that she bor-
rowed from Du Bois, who also advocated using Black ministers to promote birth control in Black communities.[84]

Some in society today have issues with preachers on the theological
Right who champion the pro-life position, but what these critics fail to
realize is that abortion in America began with preachers on the theological Left championing abortion rights. The preacher was one of the major
vehicles in Sanger's Negro Project in the '30s and in the initial stages of
spreading abortion on a much larger scale in America.

☛ **Point of Reflection:**

*Preachers leading the charge on abortion: is this a cause of cel-
ebration or shame?*

Abortion Clinics in America Established by Preachers: "The Clergy Consultation Service"

On May 22, 1967, Rev. Howard R. Moody of the Judson Memorial Church
in New York City led a group of clergy, nineteen ministers and two
rabbis, in establishing an abortion referral service at a time when abortions in America where illegal. This group of Liberal preachers posted
an article in the front page of *The New York Post* detailing their plan
to assist women in finding suitable doctors to perform abortions even
though they were illegal. In a few short years, the Clergy Consultation
Service on Abortion had referred over 100,000 women to doctors for
abortions both domestically and abroad.[85] With the success of the consultation service and the 1970 New York Law, which was the first in the
country that expanded legalized abortions for reasons other than just
the mothers health up through the first twenty-four weeks of pregnancy,

the consultation service expanded their scope and opened the first abortion clinic in the country. At this clinic thousands of abortions were performed in the years immediately preceding the Roe v Wade decision.[86] During most of the abortion movement's existence in America, there have been a group of preachers who have been very active and pivotal in advancing these goals and ideas. While some clergy who opposed abortion choose not to address the subject on the grounds that abortion is not that big of a deal, there is another contingency of clergy who have been very active in leading the charge of expanding abortion rights in America from its inception as outlined in Tom Davis's 2004 book, *Sacred Work: Planned Parenthood and Its Clergy Alliances*.[87]

Preachers have not only been active in directly advocating abortion rights; some preachers have been active in keeping the gates open on abortion due to their silence on the subject. I do not know in the modern church if there has been any other social issue that has divided clergy more than the subject of abortion. The controlling issue in terms of the church and abortion is the following: How do I interpret what the Bible has to say about pregnancy and abortion? and upon making this discovery, How should I address the issue?

Who/What Left the Gate Open on Abortion: Rejection of Scripture in Our Culture?

☛ **Point of Reflection:**

> *What does the Bible have to say about abortion: support, dissent, or indifference?*

> > Many people wrongly assume that the Bible disapproves of abortion. The truth is that abortion is not even mentioned in the Scriptures— Jewish or Christian.[88]
> > > —PPFA CLERGY ADVISORY BOARD'S
> > > PASTORAL LETTER ON ABORTION

PPFA Clergy Advisory Board's Pastoral Letter on Abortion

While the Planned Parenthood Federation of America's Clergy Advisory Board is right that the term *abortion* is not mentioned in the Bible, we have several illustrations of pregnancies and messages from God about pregnancies where we can gather a position on God's attitude on the subject. A casual glance through Scripture will reveal several examples of planned and unplanned pregnancies involving women in different stages of life and in different situations. These pregnancies involve young women, older women, poor women, unmarried women, women from minority groups, widows, women in adulterous relationships, and several other categories that Margaret Sanger and other eugenicists would consider unfit and many abortion advocates would consider prime candidates for abortion. In none of the situations do we see God condoning the decision of terminating a pregnancy. Despite this evidence for many people, the debate starts and primarily rests with when life begins.

☞ **Point of Reflection:**

When does life begin from a biblical perspective?

In Scripture we do have a clear record of God having some form of affection, communication, and concern for babies at all points during pregnancy. Below is a small sample of such scriptures.

Before conception

> Before I formed you in the belly I knew you, and before you left the womb I sanctified you; I established you as a prophet unto the nations.[89]
>
> —JEREMIAH 1:5

> The angel went to her and said, "Greetings, you who are highly favored! The Lord is with you." Mary was greatly troubled at his words and wondered what kind of greeting this might be. But the angel said to her, "Do not be afraid, Mary; you have found favor with God. You will conceive and give birth to a son, and you are to call him Jesus. He will be great and will be called the Son of the Most High. The Lord God will give him the throne of his father David, and he will reign over Jacob's descendants forever; his kingdom will never end."
>
> —LUKE 1:28–33, NIV

At the point of conception

> Then an angel of the Lord appeared to him, standing at the right side of the altar of incense. When Zechariah saw him, he was startled and was gripped with fear. But the angel said to him: "Do not be afraid, Zechariah; your prayer has been heard. Your wife Elizabeth will bear you a son, and you are to call him John. He will be a joy and delight to you, and many will rejoice because of his birth."

After this his wife Elizabeth became pregnant and for five months remained in seclusion.

—LUKE 1:11–14, 24

During pregnancy

If people are fighting and hit a pregnant woman and she gives birth prematurely but there is no serious injury, the offender must be fined whatever the woman's husband demands and the court allows.

—EXODUS 21:22, NIV

At the point of birth

The king of Egypt said to the Hebrew midwives,… "When you are helping the Hebrew women during childbirth on the delivery stool, if you see that the baby is a boy, kill him; but if it is a girl, let her live." The midwives, however, feared God and did not do what the king of Egypt had told them to do; they let the boys live. Then the king of Egypt summoned the midwives and asked them, "Why have you done this? Why have you let the boys live?" The midwives answered Pharaoh, "Hebrew women are not like Egyptian women; they are vigorous and give birth before the midwives arrive." So God was kind to the midwives and the people increased and became even more numerous. And because the midwives feared God, he gave them families of their own.

—EXODUS 1: 15–21, NIV

Anytime in Scripture where there was killing of the young or killing of babies, it always involved sin, a plague, some form of oppression, or slavery. There never was any mention in Scripture of God's approval of the discarding of babies for any reason that a parent deemed necessary. What we do have is God having concern for children at all stages of life. Regardless of whether life begins at conception; during the first, second, or third trimester; or at birth, we have clear biblical examples of God's concern, thought, communication, protection, and a plan for the child at all stages during pregnancy.

With this being the case, it would appear that God would be fully concerned about babies at all stages of pregnancy. This is what is at issue for the most part in America as it relates to abortion and the Bible. Does God sanction a woman/father/church or court having absolute authority in determining whether to terminate a pregnancy for any reason? Rape, incest, and the health of a mother are serious issues that should indeed be addressed through prayer, as well as consultation with family and spiritual guidance; but the reality in America is that none of the above three serious issues comes into play when assessing the vast majority of abortion cases in our country.[90]

As with other issues, it is one thing to make an argument about whether abortion should be legal and it is another thing to attempt to argue that the Bible validates it. To establish biblical validation for abortion, one has to invalidate each of the scriptures above in addition to the wealth of other scriptures that highlight God's concern for unborn babies and God's celebration of life. Then, once this is done, one would have to show God's indifference toward the terminating of life for any reason. One has to question after such an undertaking if support for abortion requires a perversion of the original intent of Scripture.

But in light of what the Bible has to say about the subject, in light of how it has evolved in our country, and regardless of whether anybody thinks it is right or wrong, abortions and unplanned pregnancy continue to happen in our country at a rapid pace. In determining how this issue should be addressed, it needs to be analyzed from the vantage point that abortion is a reality whether we choose to accept it or not, and we must address the issue as a reality in our world.

☞ Point of Reflection:

So should the gates swing open wider for abortion or should it start to close?

If we want the gate to remain open for abortion, then all we have to do is sit back and do nothing. With the direction that our country has been going, abortion is becoming more and more convenient and accessible, and this accessibility is being coupled with spiritual validation and/or silence from the pulpit, which is keeping the gate open. But if the gate is going to be closed on abortion, then the way of closing or curtailing this practice has to be via the same methods that were used to keep it open.

Abortion has to go from being dehumanized to humanized; the issue of life has to be infiltrated into the debate; the Supreme and federal court justices who feel that it is their role to create policies need to be replaced by justices who understand that their role is limited to interpreting the Constitution. Over the past few years, the judicial nomination process has shifted from an inquiry into the qualifications of a candidate and has focused more on an examination of the political and judicial views of a candidate. The primary issue that has taken center stage at these confirmation hearings is the issue of abortion via code words such as "respect for privacy" and "judicial precedent."

Apathy in the African American community needs to be replaced with concern and active involvement. *We need to understand that poverty and jobs are not more or less important than abortion, but are equally as important as abortion.* One does not have to suffer for the other. Margaret Sanger and her covert eugenic agenda and legacy should no longer be celebrated, and there should be a clear understanding of her motives and how her program has shaped abortion in America. Preachers should allow the Bible to guide their social involvement and understanding on this issue, as opposed to allowing society to influence how they interpret Scripture on the question of life.

The time for a silent perspective on this issue is over. Addressing abortion goes deeper than just saying that the practice is right or wrong. Addressing the issue has to involve realistic alternatives for the many women who have unplanned pregnancies, and assisting them in finding help and in providing guidance so the same mistakes do not repeat themselves.

HIV/AIDS/STDs:
Where Did They Come From and How Do We Get Rid of Them?

An Epidemic Touches a Generation

As a child of the late '70s and early '80s, I was very fortunate to have grown up in a time of the evolution in popular culture of African American athletes and music artists. In 1979 the Los Angeles Lakers drafted a sophomore, 6' 9" point guard from Michigan State University, that would have a lasting impact on sports for the next few decades. Earvin "Magic" Johnson came to the NBA when the league was searching for a fresh new image to carry them into the new decade and to rehabilitate the image and economy of the league. Wilt Chamberlain was already retired, Kareem Abdul Jabbar was aging, Michael Jordan was still in high school, and Lebron James was not yet born. The tall, young point guard with the friendly smile was perfect fit. Over the next decade he led his team to five NBA championships, earned several MVP's, and more importantly, effectively promoted his public image as not only a great athlete but an ideal role model for all children.

Around the same time a new genre of music was forming. Motown was past its heyday, the disco fad of the '70s was coming to a close, and there was a new generation of African Americans from the inner city who put together rhymes with various beats to tell their stories, painting images of their culture and their generation to the world. This blend of vocals and music was referred to as rap music or hip hop. One of the interesting trends in rap music is that although it began in New York, it quickly spread around the country and evolved into many different genres: East Coast, West Coast, and the dirty South. At the same time, many inner-city communities in the country were going through a

period of decline. These communities became characterized by gang violence, the cocaine epidemic, poor relationships with the police, broken
families, and poverty.

In Los Angeles there was a young African American teenager who
went down the unfortunate path of many in his neighborhood and began
to sell drugs and participate in gang activity. Once money came in, it was
difficult for him to walk away from the constant flow of income, so he
dropped out of school in the tenth grade. After years of selling drugs, he
transferred his street-learned occupational abilities and began to recruit
local rappers in his community to begin a rap group whose mission was
to tell the perspective of life in the inner city from firsthand accounts.
This was the beginning of another genre of rap: hardcore rap. The group
was called NWA or Niggers with an Attitude, and the brain child of this
operation was Erick "Eazy-E" Wright. He gained notoriety for his first
hit single, which would go on to become the title of a movie a few years
later, *Boyz "N" the Hood*. To some, Eazy-E was a cultural icon and to
others he was the poster child of rebellion. Before there was a Tupac, a
Biggie Smalls, or a Jay-Z, there was Eazy-E. Whatever your perspective
on Eazy-E, his music, which has sold millions of records, was not only
getting attention in Compton and Watts but in many suburban areas. It
even earned him a visit to the White House.

Magic Johnson and Eazy-E were viewed by society much differently;
one was a role model and the other was a rebel. Each of these two prominent figures in the African American community came into contact with
a deadly disease that not only changed their lives, but got the attention of
every American. We all could no longer keep quiet on the issue of HIV
and AIDS. When Magic Johnson and Eazy-E came public with revela-
tions that they had AIDS, this disease became a reality for many in my
generation. In many respects, my generation was the first in America to
experience or grow up with AIDS and a very massive outbreak of sexually
transmitted diseases across all genres, ethnicities, and income stratums.
As a young man in my early 30s, I do not know an America nor have
I been alive during a time when HIV/AIDS and Sexually Transmitted
Disease were not an epidemic in our country. To those from generations
prior to mine, maybe this may not be the story of your generation. If this
study were written forty, thirty, or possibly twenty years ago, I doubt
very seriously if this chapter would have been included. But the reality
today is that it would be impossible to do an assessment of race, faith,

and culture in this generation without discussion given to HIV/AIDS and sexually transmitted diseases in America.

What began as a quiet storm in the late '70s and early '80s has evolved into a tsunami in all of America and many places around the world. Unfortunately, some people fail to see the massive impact that HIV/AIDS and other sexually transmitted diseases are having on all facets of our culture. The reality is that this is an issue that touches all facets of American life and is just as serious as anything else in our culture. While much can and should be said on this subject, the two main questions that really get to the heart of the matter are: Where did this epidemic come from—how has it evolved in America? and Where do we go from here or how do we end or decrease it? Every other question on this subject matter positions itself under those two broad categories.

☛ **Point of Reflection:**

Are HIV/AIDS and STDs in America really that serious?

According to the Center for Disease Control, as of 2009 nearly 19 million new sexually transmitted disease infections occur each year.[1] Chlamydia is the most frequent STD reported with 1,244,180 infections reported in 2009.[2] Gonorrhea is second with 301,174 cases reported in 2009, and over the past decade there have been nearly 56,000 new HIV cases reported annually.[3] According to some estimates there are over 60 million people in America living with sexually transmitted diseases, which is roughly one out of five Americans. What these numbers reveal is that America at large has a certified sex problem that crosses all ethnicities, generations, and genders. But a casual glance through any study or statistics on STDs or specifically HIV in America will reveal that there are several groups in this country who continue to be disproportionately affected and infected by STDs. At the top of the list of those most affected by HIV are homosexual men who have sex with men. The CDC points out that although this group only represents 2 percent of the population, they are the group most severely affected by HIV and they are "the only risk group in which new HIV infections have been increasing steadily since the early 1990s." At the end of 2006, over half of all people living with HIV were men who had sex with men.[4] Though not as severely at risk, not too far behind sexually active homosexual men are African Americans at large.

STDs Among African Americans

In nearly every statistical category related to HIV and STDs, African Americans appear to be the severely at risk.

- One in sixteen Black men and one in thirty-two Black women will be diagnosed with an HIV infection at some point in their lives.[5]

- In 2009 Blacks/African Americans accounted for 52 percent of all diagnoses of HIV infection. Blacks account for nearly half of the new infections of HIV in the country.[6]

- Blacks accounted for 48 percent of persons living with HIV and 44 percent of those living with AIDS at the end of 2008.[7]

- "Blacks accounted for 71 percent of all gonorrhea cases in 2009." This is 20 percent higher than Whites.[8]

- "Blacks represented almost half of all reported chlamydia cases (48 percent) in 2009."[9]

- Blacks accounted for half of all P&S (Primary and Secondary) syphilis cases (52 percent) in 2009.[10]

While these statistics are very troubling, the reality is the problem may realistically be much worse than what is reported; not all STDs are reported to the CDC and the CDC only reports on STDs that are considered to be nationally notifiable diseases, diseases where "regular, frequent, and timely information regarding individual cases is considered necessary for the prevention and control of the disease."[11] The list is developed from voluntary reports received from State Health Departments. The CDC then in conjunction with other organizations produces summary data from these reports and updates and revises this list "periodically."[12] In other words, diseases are added and removed from the list during the review period, meaning that the true scope of STDs in America is not fully known. In order to pull the covers off, we have to start with a discussion of the origins and reasons for the spread of STDs in America. Let's use HIV/AIDS as a case study.

☛ **Point of Reflection:**

HIV/AIDS: Where did it come from?

In June of 1981 the CDC published a report, *"Pneumocystis Pneumonia—Los Angeles,"* which chronicled a pneumonia found in five unassociated gay men in three different hospitals.[13] Not too long after that reports began to appear in newspapers in New York City about a form of cancer found in forty-one gay men in New York City and around San Francisco.[14] Later reports were published that the cancerous tumor called Kaposi's Sarcoma was found in five to six new cases per week and growing at a rapid pace.[15] This disease was no longer just being found in gay men but also in heterosexuals from various parts of the country and among a group of Haitian immigrants.[16] The disease previously referred to as Gay Related Immune Deficiency and later Community Acquired Immune Deficiency eventually became more popularly referred to as Acquired Immunodeficiency Syndrome.[17] The CDC first used the term AIDS in 1982 in one of its reports. Three years later in 1985 President Reagan first mentioned AIDS at a press conference, and in 1986 the Surgeon General produced its first official report on AIDS titled *The Surgeon General's Report on Acquired Immune Deficiency Syndrome.*[18] In the months and years that followed, America and the world began to become more educated on the virus. Although the disease was initially seen by many as a gay and lesbian disease, and even today gay and lesbians are the most severely at risk, this disease impacts everyone.[19] The 1986 Surgeon General Report revealed that there was a variety of ways the virus could be transmitted, but the two most common methods for contracting the virus is by sharing syringe needles or by sexual relations.[20] From the late '80s to the early '90s there were a variety of celebrities who had become infected and some went public with the revelation of their contact with this disease.

In 1997 the independent non-profit organization, The Institute of Medicine's Committee on the Prevention and Control of Sexually Transmitted Diseases, published a book called *The Hidden Epidemic: Confronting Sexually Transmitted Diseases.* In the book the committee spends nearly a chapter dealing with some of the social factors that led to the spread and evolution of sexually transmitted diseases in America.[21] The committee identified poverty and inadequate resources as the key social factors in spreading STDs. They argued that "groups with the poorest access to healthcare" as well as "disenfranchised groups" have some of the highest rates of STDs and are disproportionally affected by STDs.[22] There are groups, according to the report, with little political influence who are very impoverished and difficult to reach.[23] The committee also pointed out the role of the media in framing ideas about sex and its impact on STDs in America.[24]

> Americans, especially adolescents, receive unbalanced mass media messages about sexuality, sexual behavior, and sexual responsibility. Premarital sex, cohabitation, and non-marital relationships are depicted as the norm for adults.[25]

The study went on to say:

> Although sex is frequently portrayed on television, protective behavior is rarely shown and references to adverse consequences are rare; casual unprotected intercourse is presented as the norm.[26]

This report lends itself to much larger issues in America in terms of the impact of society's evolving views on sex directly corresponding with the spread of STDs in America. These evolving mores and attitudes about sex go back to the mid '60s during the period of time I refer to as the Liberation Generation.

Sexually Transmitted Diseases: A Direct Descendent of the Liberation Generation[27]

The culture, actions, and practices of each generation are in many ways a direct response to the decisions made by the previous generation. It can easily be detected that civil rights and voting rights in the '60s led to an increase in Black elected officials in the '80s, '90s and 2000s; and it should also be easy to see that sex liberation in the '60s and '70s paved the way for STDs and HIV in the '80s, '90s, and 2000s.

Sex liberation was every bit of a pillar of the Liberation Generation; sex liberation was just as influential in shaping America in the '60s and '70s as Black liberation, women's liberation, and drug liberation. Sex liberation was seen in movies, music, television, attire, and politics. One of the clearest examples that America's attitudes about sex and sexuality was evolving was the findings in 1970 of the Presidential Commission on Obscenity and Pornography.[28] In 1967 President Lyndon Johnson formed a commission to study the impact of pornography on society in America and the potential constitutional and legal challenges with establishing policies to control distribution of pornography. The commission found that pornography did not have a negative impact on adults, nor did it hinder or have a negative impact on moral behavior, attitudes, or sexual conduct. The report did not favor putting laws in place that limited or attempted to control the distribution of pornographic material.[29] The report was released in 1970 when President Nixon was in office. A few weeks after its release, President Nixon stated, "I categorically reject its morally bankrupt conclusions and major recommendations."[30] He also stated, "The Commission on Pornography and Obscenity has performed a disservice, and I totally reject its report."[31]

Unfortunately this report, along with the 1969 U.S. Supreme Court decision Stanley v. Georgia which ruled that "the first and fourteenth amendments prohibit making mere private possession of obscene material a crime,"[32] created an executive and judicial platform for the evolving sexual liberation to stand on. It was almost a decade after the findings of the commission that the CDC released its first report on what would become HIV/AIDS. While I *am not* suggesting that the Supreme Court decision and findings of the commission in and of itself was the sole cause of HIV/AIDS and expanding STDs in America, I *am* suggesting that the high court decision and findings of the committee helped to provide a firm legal foundation upon which sexual liberation in America could be built. Today the selling, marketing, and celebration of undisciplined sexual behavior has become a normal part of our culture. It would be impossible to discuss or deal with how to effectively address sexually transmitted diseases without there being a focus on *sex*.

Drugs, Poverty, and Undisciplined Sex: STDs Unholy Trinity!

While sex is and has been the primary method for contracting HIV, one of the other ways this virus has been frequently transmitted is through injection drug use via sharing of syringe needles. According to the CDC, once the virus has been transmitted, people who have sex with injection drug users (IDU) are also at risk for infection.[33] Injection drug use by both heterosexuals and homosexuals continues to be the second leading cause of HIV transmission in America,[34] and again African Americans are disproportionately impacted. They account for over 50 percent of IDUs who contracted HIV and over 50 percent of IDUs that are living with AIDS.[35]

Unfortunately, the unholy linkage between drugs and STDs are not just limited to drugs that can be ingested via syringes but also involve non-injection drugs such as cocaine and crack cocaine. According to a report from the CDC, non-injection drug users also help to spread the virus through trading sex for drugs and/or money and participating in "risky sexual behaviors."[36] This is another sad reality in many low-income neighborhoods; prostitution for drug money is a common occurrence. In neighborhoods where drugs are being bought and sold frequently, prostitution is one of the most common methods for female and some male drug users to acquire money to support their habits. In the process they contract and spread sexually transmitted diseases. Even on a broader level, a recent CDC report found:

> Poverty is the single most important demographic factor associated with HIV infection among inner-city heterosexuals. Contrary to severe racial disparities that characterize the overall U.S. epidemic, researchers found no differences in HIV prevalence by race/ethnicity in this population.[37]

Poverty leads to HIV due to individuals having "limited access to quality health care, housing, and HIV prevention education."[38] So what we have in America as it relates to the spread of STDs is poverty, drugs, and unhealthy sexual practices, with each having some degree of impact on the spread of STDs.

☛ **Points of Reflection:**

Does poverty lead to increased drug use and increased sexual activity?

Does drug addiction lead to poverty and unhealthy sexual practices?

Does an unhealthy sexual appetite lead to drugs or help to enable poverty?

While it is uncertain as to which of the three is the more dominant variable, we do understand that each has predominantly filtered into unhealthy sexual practices. While there have been various methods and perspectives on how to attack the problem of STDs, at the core of the problem is sex, so this is where solutions ought to begin.

☛ **Point of Reflection:**

STDs, where do we go from here: how do we attack the problem?

The Issue is Sex

As discussed in Question 4, there is a common belief in America among many on the Left and Right about a strong apprehension of the

government getting involved in and taking a position on private sex decisions, yet this apprehension is coupled with the belief that the government should be very active in fighting, controlling, and in some cases
eliminating some STDs. Most governmental attempts to address STDs
really have not been targeted to the issue of *sex* but have focused more
on the economic, social, public policy, psychological, and scientific issues
involved with the spread of these diseases. A truly comprehensive plan
must indeed involve all of these factors in the prevention of new cases
of HIV and in assisting the millions of Americans who already have
STDs, as expressed in the CDC's HIV Prevention Strategic Plan and
the National HIV/AIDS Strategy for the United States. However, there
have to be some direct attempts or discussions on the role of sex and
the values associated with it in our society. This has to be the launching
point in the discussion. If the government is apprehensive about taking
on this challenge, then this is an area of great opportunity for the church.

☛ **Point of Reflection:**

> *The political Left initiated the war on poverty; the political Right
> initiated the war on drugs: who is going to initiate the war on
> undisciplined sexual behavior to address STDs?*

Here is where I think it is absurdity to attempt to exclude any form
of discussion on morality or faith from the public square. If what is at
issue with STDs is sex, than how can this issue be addressed without
some form of moral construct to frame the discussion. In July 2010 the
Obama Administration released its National HIV/AIDS Strategy for the
United States, in which it argued that to address this issue, a more coor-
dinated effort was needed. The report states, "Success will require the
commitment of governments at all levels, businesses, faith communities,
philanthropy, the scientific and medical communities, educational institutions, people living with HIV, and others."[39] One of the goals outlined
in the National HIV/AIDS Strategy is reducing the number of new HIV
infections.[40] One of the methods that this plan identifies is to "expand
targeted efforts to prevent HIV infection using a combination of effective, evidence-based approaches."[41] According to the report they list
the following "scientifically proven bio-medical and behavioral based
approaches":[42]

- Abstinence from Sex or Drug Use

- HIV Testing

- Condom Availability

- Access to Sterile Needles and Syringes

- HIV Treatment

The report mentions that there is no "single magic-bullet" or isolated method to address this problem and encourages using multiple efforts to address the problem.[43] Despite the plea for a multiplicity of approaches, the one approach that grants a "foolproof" way of eliminating the spread of and instances of new STD infections has come under *by far* the most scrutiny and is the least used while the other methods listed arguably have become the primary tools in addressing the issue. Most HIV and STD prevention programs fall under two fundamental premises; methods geared toward abstaining from practices that lead to HIV and STD transmission or methods geared toward reducing risk when engaging in practices that can lead to STD and HIV prevention.

Safe Sex/Safe Drug Use vs. Drug-Free and Abstinence Programs

☛ **Point of Reflection:**

Just say no and Abstinence-only programs: Are they worth the investment?

If practiced, abstaining from sex and drug use is by far the most effective way of reducing HIV infections and STD transmissions. In the 1980s former First Lady Nancy Reagan told my generation, Just Say No! This overall message was coupled with programs such as the Los Angeles Police Department's Drug Abuse Resistance Education and policies such as the Adolescent Family Life Act (AFLA), which had a primary emphasis of encouraging abstinence via research, developing programs, and providing grants to organizations that developed curricula focused on abstaining from sex. Although the main focus of the AFLA was to discourage teens from sexual relationships outside the confines of marriage, the program also provided assistance to teens who were pregnant or already had children.[44] Then in the mid 1990s the Personal Responsibility and Work Opportunity Act (know as the Welfare Reform Act) was signed into law, which amended Title V of the Social Security Act and placed greater emphasis on federally funded abstinence-only programs. This bill established eight guidelines that all federally funded abstinence programs had to include.[45]

1. Has as its exclusive purpose teaching the social, psychological, and health gains to be realized by abstaining from sexual activity

2. Teaches abstinence from sexual activity outside marriage as expected standard for all school-age children

3. Teaches that abstinence from sexual activity is the only certain way to avoid out-of-wedlock pregnancy, sexually transmitted diseases, and other associated health problems

4. Teaches that a mutually faithful monogamous relationship in the context of marriage is the expected standard of human sexual activity

5. Teaches that sexual activity outside of the context of marriage is likely to have harmful psychological and physical affects

6. Teaches that bearing children out-of-wedlock is likely to have harmful consequences for the child, the child's parents, and society

7. Teaches young people how to reject sexual advances and how alcohol and drug use increases vulnerability to sexual advances

8. Teaches the importance of attaining self-sufficiency before engaging in sexual activity

This policy readjusted the focus of abstinence education by showing the strong benefits of abstinence and the serious consequences that many adolescents experience when they have children out of wedlock. In 2000 Congress created the Community-Based Abstinence Education program (CBAE), which awarded money directly to private and non-profit organizations who administered abstinence-only education per the guidelines in the Title 5 Social Security Act. While society continues to reject abstinence as being unrealistic, it really has been the only biblical perspective on the issue of sex outside of marriage.

Abstinence or abstinence-only education, as it is frequently labeled, focuses its message on telling students the many challenges that are associated with being sexually active outside of marriage. Most public drug and sex-free programs are rooted in a strong faith-based foundation, which continues to be a stumbling block for strong opponents of the government being involved in anything remotely faith-based.

Organizations such as the Sexuality Information and Education Council of the United States (SIECUS), Planned Parenthood, Advocates for Youth, and The American Civil Liberties Union (ACLU) have consistently led the charge in attacks on abstinence-only education. From ACLU's failed lawsuit, Bowen v. Kendrick, where the ACLU argued that the AFLA violated the first amendment principle of separation between church and state[46] to its present-day rhetoric, the ACLU has been on a crusade to end abstinence-only education. Recently they argued in a newsletter encouraging its supporters to oppose federal funding of abstinence-only education:

> By excluding information about safe sex practices and teaching about sex only in the context of marriage, abstinence-only programs stigmatize gay and lesbian teens and undermine efforts to educate them on HIV and STD prevention. Many abstinence-only curricula are overtly hostile to lesbians and gay men. Such hostility violates the rights of these students to attend school free of discrimination."[47]

It is one thing to say that abstinence-only programs may not be as effective as other programs, *which is very debatable*, but it is another thing to say that abstinence-only programs should be banned. Here lies the fundamental difference of opinion and more broadly the fundamental difference in worldview. If teaching children to abstain from drug use and to abstain from sex outside of marriage is inherently wrong, discriminatory, or against popular culture in America, then the problem of HIV/AIDS and STDs is much deeper than just a viral epidemic. Rather, it suggests a morally and culturally deficient epidemic that also needs massive attention.

Outside of the moral disagreements with abstinence and drug-free programs, some will contend that abstinence-only and drug-free programs are not as efficient as programs that encourage safe sex and safe drug use or what they label as "comprehensive sex education." They contend that there is no scientific proof that these programs work; once again the ACLU articulates the dissent:

> Research has shown, again and again, that lecturing young people
> to "just say no to sex before marriage" does not prevent pregnancy
> or sexually transmitted diseases. It merely denies students impor-
> tant information they need to be safe and healthy. *Even worse,*
> abstinence-only education uses medically inaccurate information—
> *lies*—to scare students. ... But eliminating the federal dollars behind
> abstinence-only education won't rid our schools of it. We need to do
> that, together, in school communities throughout the Bay Area.[48]

The almost continuous attacks against abstinence-only education have
centered on there being an alleged lack of scientific study to establish a
sufficient need for the programs; but there have been a series of reports
in the last few years to establish that abstinence education is a valuable
and efficient tool in addressing STDs and HIV in America. A 2009 study
funded by the Department of Health and Human Services found that
"approximately 70 percent of parents surveyed are opposed to pre-marital
sex both in general and for their own adolescents."[49] This study found
that "the majority of parents surveyed favor their adolescents receiving
abstinence messages from multiple sources."[50] While the study did find
some distinctions based upon religious affiliation and age of adolescents,
overall the report found that "parents and adolescents generally oppose
pre-marital sex."[51]

In addition, a 2010 report conducted by the University of Pennsylvania
that targeted African American youth found that "theory-based abstinence-only interventions may have an important role in preventing adolescent sexual involvement."[52] This report, which was considered by the
Washington Post as "game-changing,"[53] was "the first randomized controlled trial to demonstrate that an abstinence-only intervention reduced
the percentage of adolescents who reported any sexual intercourse for a
long period following the intervention."[54] These were two classic criticisms of abstinence education that this report disproved: (1) that it did
not lead to sustained results and (2) that it was never proven effective.
While this report did not meet the A–H federal guidelines of abstinence education as established in the Welfare Reform Act, it did show
that there is clear evidence that abstinence programs are effective and
valuable in deterring sex among youth, thereby preventing STDs. These
studies provide an element of scientific validation for abstinence education that many continue to be very weary of our federal government
financially supporting.

☛ **Point of Reflection:**

If the federal government should not teach abstinence-only programs, then should federal government even be involved in the discussion?

While drug-free and abstinence programs have been targets of consistent attacks and criticism, some have favored programs that *reduce* the risk of STD transmission as opposed to eliminating the risk.

Comprehensive Sex Education and Needle-Exchange Programs

In July of 2009 Congress and President Obama allowed funding to expire for Title V (A–H) abstinence-only education and later in the year ended federal funding for Community-Based Abstinence Education (CBAE) and abstinence programs associated with the Adolescent Family Life Act (AFLA).[55] These cuts and expirations ultimately ended both CBAE and the abstinence portion of AFLA and brought an overall end to federal funding for abstinence-only education.[56] Funding for Title V would eventually be restored the following year through a compromise by the president and Congress to get health care reform passed.[57] The actions of Congress and the president led in many ways to the climax of an almost thirty-year battle to end federal funding for abstinence-only education and to replace it with "morally neutral" programs that did not place as strong of an emphasis on the benefits of drug-free and abstinence education. Detractors have argued that federal funding and attention should be placed on programs that do not have as strong of a moral tone, and are allegedly more realistic in addressing HIV/STD prevention; two of the main programs in this mold are comprehensive sex education and needle-exchange programs.

Harm-Reduction Programs

In the same appropriations bill that ended federal funding for abstinence-only education, Congress and the president adopted a different path that lifted a twenty-year ban on federal funding for needle-exchange programs.[58] Around the same time President Obama, via the Surgeon General of the United States, made a determination that needle-exchange programs were effective tools in "reducing drug abuse," and its programs were eligible for federal block grants.[59] In many respects these programs expanded a federal government departure from seeking to discourage injection drug use to adopting *harm- reduction* practices that now seek to provide safe measures for those who participate in illegal and harmful processes.

Harm reduction is a body of programs that are based on the premise that there will "never be a drug free society,"[60] and therefore, a variety of methods are implemented to reduce the harm associated with drug use. According to the Drug Policy Alliance, "every solution with the potential to help should be considered."[61] Harm reduction includes programs such as "Supervised Injection Facilities,"[62] which are government supported, medically supervised, and safe locations where pre-obtained drugs can be used. While America has yet to adopt this method of harm reduction, which some organizations in our country strongly support, the federal government has embraced another more popular version of harm reduction: needle-exchange programs.

Needle-Exchange Programs

In the early 1980s in the City of Rotterdam, trade unions were formed to represent the needs and health concerns of hard drug users; this group referred to themselves as the "Junkiebond."[63] As the ideas of this group spread around the Netherlands, a group of addicts in Amsterdam began to develop a strong concern about dirty needle use among their peers. In order to help address this issue, the members of the Junkiebond would collect the dirty needles and syringes and would exchange them for clean ones. This method of disease control was the first needle-exchange program.[64] A few years later a former drug user and at the time current graduate student at Yale University, Jon Parker, began meeting with drug users in New Haven, Connecticut, to inform them of the high relationship between using unclean needles and acquiring diseases. During one of his meetings, one the drug users brought in sterilized needles and distributed them to the others in attendance. In November of 1986 Jon began to exchange needles in the New Haven community, and his efforts have quickly spread around the country.[65] A few years later in 1989 the Tacoma-Pierce County Board of Health in Tacoma, Washington, approved funding for a needle-exchange program, which was initiated by David Purchase, a man who began a one-man crusade of handing out clean needles in Tacoma. The City of Tacoma became the first organized and government recognized needle-exchange program in America.[66] According to the *North American Syringe Exchange Network,* as of

2009 there are 211 needle-exchange programs in over thirty-six states.[67] Some of the programs are legal and some are not. Some are run by public health clinics, and some are run by individuals riding around a city and distributing clean needles out of a car or van.[68] The underlying premise of this program, according to its advocates, is not to discourage drug use but rather to provide a way where it can be done safely.[69] The proponents of this program are quick to inform the public that based upon various research from government and nongovernment agencies, the data reveals that this program does not increase or encourage the use of drugs and that some of the organizations who administer this program also connect drug users to drug prevention programs.[70] While the needle-exchange program may not encourage drug use, it certainly does not discourage it nor does it discuss the many negative consequences of drug use besides HIV transmission.

Needle-exchange programs, like most of the other harm-reduction, morally-neutral programs, appear to be so firm in their commitment of not inserting any form of morality into the discussion that they have no problem with supporting individuals as they actively participate in programs that lead to their demise. If the federal government has adopted needle-exchange programs, then it is not farfetched to say that "Supervised Injection Facilities" will naturally follow.

☛ **Point of Reflection:**

   At what point if any should the federal government inject some idea of right and wrong (morality) into public policy?

Comprehensive Sex Education

☛ **Point of Reflection:**

Abstinence-only or abstinence-plus education: the dilemma of comprehensive sex education?

In many respects, comprehensive sex education is an older cousin of needle exchanges and supervised injection facilities in terms of harm reduction programs. The fundamental premise of comprehensive sex education is not to discourage premarital sex or place any form of moral position associated with premarital sex, but rather to present a series of methods associated with minimizing the risk of contracting a sexually transmitted disease. According to the Advocates for Youth, one of the major distinctions between abstinence-only education and comprehensive education is to "deliver and consistently reinforce a clear message about abstaining from sexual activity and/or using condoms or other forms of contraception."[71]

☛ **Point of Reflection:**

How can one effectively advocate abstinence while distributing condoms?

Most literature on comprehensive sex education appears to be inundated with consistent attacks against abstinence-only education. It is almost as if one of the goals of comprehensive sex education is to refute the major arguments of abstinence-only education. Comprehensive sex education advocates contend that abstinence education is based on fear tactics;[72] and that it is ineffective, unethical, poor public health;[73] and the list goes on and on. According to this philosophy, abstinence should be one in a series of methods, which includes contraception, to affectively address STD transmissions. It really begs the question: If both programs allegedly have a commitment to abstinence, then why is there such a big problem with programs that exclude contraception?

I remember my days in high school where the health class instructor took her two fingers and instructed the class on how to properly use condoms and how it was understood that if anyone ever needed condoms, they could safely and confidentially retrieve them from the health clinic. Yet I have no memory of there ever being any discussion on the benefits of abstinence and the legitimate consequences of premarital sex. One has to wonder how aggressively, if at all, abstinence is being taught in comprehensive programs if the teaching is coupled with contraception. While this endless debate can go on in the public sector, when the discussion is turned to Scripture in terms of how to effectively address HIV and STDs, we find more definitive language.

HIV/AIDS/STDs and the Church

In analyzing an effective church response for HIV and AIDS, I am reminded of a life-changing encounter that I had in Atlanta a few years ago. As I was coming out of a famous restaurant in Atlanta after a wonderful meal, a homeless man came up to me and asked if he could have a dollar; so I reached in my pocket a gave him one. Another homeless man saw what happened from across the street where he was sitting and rushed over and asked if he could also have a dollar; so I gave it to him as well. All of a sudden out of nowhere there were at least fifteen to twenty men that came near me asking for dollars; and I gave each of them a dollar until I was out of money in my pocket. After distributing money, I took all of the men aside and began to share with them the gospel and pray with them corporately on the street corner.

As the group began to disperse and I began to get in my car, a man came running up to me crying. He said, "Sir, you have to help me." This middle aged, very slender man with tears dripping from his face said, "I have full-blown AIDS. I have had it for nearly seventeen years and I need help." At this point he showed me his arms, which appeared to be covered with bumps and scars all over. In addition, he had a series of open wounds on his arm with fluid discharging from the wounds, and he continued to say, "You got to help me; you got to help me." My heart was torn to pieces standing on the street corner staring at a frail man weeping, whose life was sinking in the ravages of poverty, pain, and AIDS. The compassion in me wanted to give him a hug, go to the nearest ATM, and give him as much money as I could; but wisdom dictated that neither would have been smart decisions. It was obvious that his concerns and needs superseded the dollar that he was asking for. Here was a dying, homeless, poor man; and the question that ran through my mind during my encounter with him, and that continued for the weeks and months that followed, was: What hope was there for him?

What could I do, and more broadly, what could and should the church do to help him? I assume that his challenges needed systematic attention that would involve more than just a drive-by solution. While I never asked him nor was I concerned at the time with the cause of his predicament, I did understand that the healing this man needed was physical, psychological, emotional, and spiritual. The primary venue where such holistic healing and help could take place for this man and others in his position, and a series of other people who are only a few bad decisions away from his predicament, are places of faith. That's what they were created for. Regardless of any governmental reform, the manner in which the church treats the wounded and afflicted is the best barometer of how society and culture will follow.

QUESTION 6: HIV/AIDS/STDs:
Where Did They Come From and How Do We Get Rid of Them?

143

STDs/HIV and AIDS:
How Does the Bible Prescribe Addressing STDs?

There is no scripture in the Bible that deals directly with AIDS or HIV; however, there is a wealth of information in Scripture on the leading cause of AIDS/HIV and STDs, which is consensual sex. A case can be made (though not explicitly stated) that there are instances of diseases associated with lascivious behavior in Scripture. One possible example is the story of a woman with an issue of blood which is recorded in the Synoptic Gospels; Matthew (9:20–22), Mark (5:24–33), and Luke (8:43–48). While the Bible does not tell us the cause or the exact nature of her issue of blood, her predicament has striking similarities with the man I encountered in Atlanta and the many people who are living with HIV/AIDS in America. This story provides a biblical strategy for addressing the issue.

When this woman was introduced in Scripture, we see Jesus in the middle of having a very urgent and serious encounter with a man whose daughter is at the point of death. Jesus, as was and is His custom, made a commitment to the man that He would attend to his ailing daughter. At this point in Jesus' life, He was in his first year of ministry and was dealing with the challenges of presenting His doctrine of "love and compassion" to the current religious sect which was characterized by "law and order." The country in which Jesus lived was dealing with the challenges of racism and classism, which was an unfortunate part of their culture that Jesus also sought to address. On His way to the man's house who had the ailing daughter at the point of death, a large crowd began to follow Jesus as His fame and notoriety began to spread. Then all of a sudden, unexpectedly and abruptly, a woman very aggressively grabs hold of Jesus' clothes and Jesus' attention now shifts from all of the other challenges He is facing toward this rather aggressive woman who is having a very serious issue with blood discharging from her body.

In many ways, this picture is the story of America in the early 1980s when HIV and AIDS were first introduced in our culture. As a nation, we faced urgent economic challenges which were characterized by high unemployment rates and rising debt. There were troubled relationships abroad with the Cold War in the former Soviet Union and very tense relationships in the Middle East. As a nation, we were only fifteen to twenty years removed from de jure segregation and discrimination; and in many parts of the country de facto segregation and discrimination were still very active. There was also a change in leadership philosophy from Carter's Progressivism to Reagan's Conservatism, which adjusted how challenges were addressed in our culture. And with the same passion and sense of urgency that the woman in the story grabbed hold of Jesus' garment in the crowd in the middle of all of the other challenges that were going on at this time, HIV and AIDS hit the American culture in the early '80s like a thief in the night who came in subtly. When its full impact was made, every community in America would experience its impact.

The implicit dilemma in the scripture is what Jesus was going to do. He was already in pursuit of a dying, young, innocent girl, and he was faced with a series of other cultural challenges in His generation; but He gets confronted with a woman who possibly has a self-inflicted wound. Due to her condition, she was legally excommunicated from culture. She was viewed as unclean and was not allowed to have any form of contact with anyone during her period of her intense bleeding which has lasted for twelve years. This is one of the many dilemmas of HIV and AIDS in America that some have trouble with. With all of the other health and economic challenges in our country, should America shift its attention from all of the other challenges that the nation is going through in order to focus on a new problem or issue that was and is affecting our country, due in large part to personal indulgences?

In the early 1980s people with HIV and AIDS were treated in the same manner that this woman in Scripture was treated: almost complete and total excommunication from everyone in society. This fear of the unknown and ostracism toward those with HIV and AIDS led many to question how the church or government should address this most urgent issue. To some, addressing HIV and AIDS is not a matter of assisting those who are afflicted but rather it is a matter of neglecting others who are allegedly more deserving (those with diseases that are not self-inflicted). HIV/AIDS and STDs have not been treated with the same level of concern as diabetes and cancer in America (this is not to suggest that diabetes can be caused in the same way). The fundamental difference in perspective is in large part due to the cause of the ailment. However, the example that Jesus gives us is that one does not have to suffer for the other. When it comes to assisting hurting people, Jesus' compassion has never been stifled by the factors leading up to the cause of one's predicament. Jesus consistently blends love and compassion with accountability; His concern for a person never validated bad decisions or avoided accountability. In reverse, His championing of accountability and self-responsibility never hampered His compassion for hurting people.

What is ironic about this story is that the Bible records that at the time when this lady had an encounter with Jesus, she was suffering with her condition for twelve years, or a little over a decade, before her condition got to a place where it was completely unbearable. The Bible states that this woman had exhausted all of her resources on medical care, which ultimately could not help her. On top of being sick, she now was poor. It is interesting that studies have found that a person can live with AIDS untreated for about a decade, and while there have been advances in medicine to address HIV and AIDS, the reality is there is no cure for the disease. Many people who have been infected with the virus are impoverished and lack the resources to effectively treat the disease, which would at best extend their lives and not eliminate the virus. This lack of cost-efficient medical treatment has caused some to just give up, and they have lost all hope.

The turning point in this woman's life was when she made the decision to turn to Jesus. Jesus was not bound by any moral constraints that hindered His ability to effectively address her situation despite what others thought about her; and Jesus made the determination not to neglect this woman in her hurting hour, despite what others may have thought. And He stopped what He was doing and gave His full attention to the hurting woman. While HIV and AIDS may be a stumbling block for many in our culture today, this is an issue that the church must speak to practically, financially, and more importantly, morally and ethically. One of the other challenges that our nation is facing with HIV and AIDS is the desire to address this issue yet maintain great passivity on taking any moral position on the factors that lead to HIV and AIDS. Any church involvement on the subject of HIV/AIDS and/or STDs has to be coupled with some form of discussion or treatment of the issue of sex.

While there are many different perspectives on issues surrounding sex in America, the biblical perspective can be summed up into two words: "Flee fornication" (1 Cor. 6:18). While there is little room for ambiguity in this statement, the concern that people have is that while this passage is clear, we also have to take into account the reality that many people are very sexually active and do not abide by this standard. We must deal with the reality; but do we lower or change the biblical standard to deal with the reality of sex in America?

☞ **Point of Reflection:**

The Bible says fornication and adultery are sins, yet many people do not adhere to it; what should the church do?

In many respects this discussion has come down to classic ethical and theological debates. Some factions of the church have taken the position that many outside the church have taken. As opposed to trying to teach and encourage abstinence, they suggest that the church should adopt harm-reduction strategies. This belief holds that condoms should be distributed at "houses of worship and faith-based educational settings."[74] As advocated recently by a major denomination, this philosophy is indirectly arguing that the church's teaching of abstinence is not effective.

☞ **Point of Reflection:**

Is the message of abstinence in the church ineffective or untested?

Arguably, the church has drifted further and further away from Orthodox beliefs and practices in America, so the message of abstaining from sexually deviant behavior would seem to be *abandoned* as opposed to *ineffective*. When churches who represent the moral backbone of our culture are suggesting handing out condoms in church, one has to wonder the commitment level to the message of abstinence in places of worship.

Spreading the message of abstinence would have to involve more than just talking points in a sermon or Bible study, but rather would include programs, organizations, support groups, significant resources, training programs for parents and teens, and church and community wide campaigns, etc., focused on this message with realistic targets and goals. There would have to be a major campaign from the church geared toward the message of abstinence for it to be effective in our culture, which is dominated by diverse messages on sex and sexuality.

The church has full access to the one tool that the government does not have and that the framers of the constitution worked hard to make sure that the churches never lost. This tool was the ability to express morality unencumbered. The First Amendment of the Constitution states, "Congress shall make no law respecting an establishment of religion, or prohibiting the free exercise thereof." In other words, Congress or the government does not have the authority to interfere with the church's expression of morality. The framers of the Constitution wanted the

church to be able to speak unencumbered to issues facing each new generation without the restrictions of the government. If there is any hope
for there being any true resolution to HIV and AIDS in our culture, the
church has to take advantage of its moral obligation and constitutional
right to speak to the issue effectively, strategically, passionately, and with
a heart of love and compassion in guiding our nation out of this mess.

Just as with the woman in the story, everything in her life changed
when she reached out to her representation of faith, which was Jesus. The
answers to our problems will be found when America as a nation dis-
covers that it is time to reach out and hold on to faith.

SECTION III
THE NEW DIRECTION

Question 7

WHERE DO WE GO FROM HERE?

A three-stranded cord is not easily broken.
—ECCLESIASTES 4:12, CJB

Compassion, Conviction, Courage

WHAT WE FIND in our present culture, and in our study, is that African Americans have become identified as people of compassion. This compassion has been expressed in a love for all people; concern for the least of these; and advocates for equality, justice, diversity, and fairness. Christians in our present culture have become identified as people of conviction—people who have expressed the ability to stand for principles that are believed regardless of their popularity or social acceptances. My contention is not that African Americans exclusively embrace compassion or that Christians exclusively embrace conviction, but rather these are the dominant variables that both groups more closely identify with in our current political and social environment. The dilemma that appears to exist with African American Christians is with balance.

To some, conviction is viewed as the enemy of compassion and compassion is seen as stifling conviction. This dilemma is manifested politically, culturally, and spiritually in our society, with the greatest tension being seen in applying race and faith or compassion and conviction to some of the serious issues facing our generation. It would appear that attitudes on each of the questions addressed in this study, as well as several others, are skewed either in the direction of conviction or in the direction of compassion. When I hear some in our society, in an attempt to celebrate diversity, easily discard and invalidate certain areas of Scripture to promote unity, I can see compassion but I see a deficit of conviction. When I see others in society who, in bouts of frustration with the economic challenges in our country, argue that those in society who do not pay taxes and are near the bottom are free riders and should not have a vote on certain economic conditions, I can hear conviction but I see a void of compassion. The new direction that I advocate culturally, socially, and politically, is a direction that effectively balances the two in addressing the challenges in our society. In addressing these challenges there would appear to be only one effective element that could bridge the massive gap between compassion and conviction; and that is courage.

Courage in its purest sense is a product of compassion and conviction. Courage is the ability to effectively blend morality with justice. Courage is the understanding that accountability does not mean animosity, and that concern may not always lead to concession or consensus. Courage is the ability to effectively address the challenges in our society dualistically; with a passion that is rooted in compassion, and a care and concern that is rooted in our conviction. The hallmark scripture in the Bible, John 3:16, speaks to this dualism in perspective; the same God who loves and has compassion for the world is the same God who speaks about the possibility of perishing or demise. This is possibly one of the most effective ways in charting a new direction.

Courage in politics is the ability of leaders to do what is in the best interest of the people, regardless of whether or not it steps outside the boundaries of their partisan position. Courage in the pulpit is the ability to maintain the integrity of one's spiritual assignment by not backing away from challenging the cultural and social norms of the day. Courage understands that there is a time to remain quiet and there is time to speak out; and on a consistent basis spiritual leaders should position themselves to be a counsel to political leaders while not compromising their spiritual and prophetic responsibility.

So it is with compassion and conviction that I courageously outline a few recommendations for African American Christians in addressing the challenges in society.

Balance Biblical Integrity, Social Consciousness, and Racial Equality

In the Question 1 of the book, I presented a survey of various theological paradigms and how they filtered into various social and political worldviews. The reality is when looking at race, faith, and politics, many African American born-again Christians' theological paradigm, although rooted in Fundamentalism, may have *some* elements of the other theologies presented. As illustrated in Question 1, African American born-again Christians identify at large with Fundamentalism's views on the integrity, authority, and infallibility of Scripture. Yet voting trends make a case that African American born-again Christians also agree with the Social Gospel's willingness to aggressively use theology to address injustices in society, while also acknowledging the need to have a candid dialogue on race relations in the church, government/politics, and culture. More often than not, one of these three commitments tends to overshadow the others.

So, the opportunity presented to African American born-again Christians is balancing biblical integrity, social consciousness, and racial equality in politics and popular culture. This arguably is the biblical example that Christ established and encourages for His followers in bridging the gap between race, faith, and politics. Throughout Christ's ministry, He was resolute in defending and living according to scriptural standards; at the same time He never allowed His commitment to Scripture to blind Him to the injustices of His current generation and He consistently communicated with and established relationships with people from other ethnicities. This is the racial, biblical, and cultural challenge of this generation; doing what Christ did in regards to these three issues.

Become Partisan Hybrids (if Necessary)

Biblical consistency is political uncertainty

The views and opinions of most people are very diverse, and rarely if ever will perfectly fit into a party's platform. So, the challenge is being an active member (consistently voting for) of a political party, while remaining true to core values even if they go against the norms of that party. To deal with these challenges, I suggest that it is OK to remain a member of a political party, if you choose to do so, as long as you do not cave in *or remain silent on* beliefs that you find to be important, regardless of whether or not they are in the main stream of that party. Now at some point a reassessment should be given if you consistently find yourself at odds with a party that you have supported for many years. At this point you do need to reconsider why you are consistently voting for a party that does not speak to the challenges in society from the perspective that you agree with. While some use the argument of "the lesser of two evils," at some point even that argument needs to be reassessed; and there should be pressure placed on leadership in that party to readjust their thinking or the solution may be for you to jump ship.

But there have been several strong examples of people who remained in political parties, yet they did not fear to take a strong stand on issues that they believed in, even if it was in opposition to the core tenets of the party.

Bob Casey Sr.

A former governor of Pennsylvania, a major state in terms of national politics, was a lifelong Democrat yet he was a strong voice in the pro-life movement. At one point, he was at the center of a Supreme Court case in the 1980s not long after the Roe v Wade decision based upon his strong pro-life position.

Colin Powell

In the mid 1990s there was a strong belief in the country that Colin Powell was going to be the first Black president. He was a Republican who served in both Democrat and Republican administrations. In 1996 on prime time television Colin Powell stated at the Republican National Convention that he "strongly supported Affirmative Action." While that position, which he never kept quiet, drew boos from the crowd, he has remained a well respected voice in both parties.

Pastor E.V. Hill

E.V. Hill was a Baptist preacher from Los Angeles, who could be considered a community activist and moral leader who had influence throughout America. Dr. Hill has deep roots in the Civil Rights movement and was a close ally of many leaders in the African American Social Gospel movement, yet during the '70s and '80s he also became one of the few black voices in religious right circles. This was a man who in 1984 was an early supporter and organizer of Jesse Jackson's presidential campaign, yet at the same time he was also a close friend of Jerry Falwell and ministered at his church. Dr. Hill's message and actions indeed represented a balanced and effective biblical perspective, in that he was able to have compassion on the least of these, speak out against social evils in society, not abandon his identity with African American culture and yet be well respected by both Black and White Christians from both theological and political perspectives. What makes this astonishing is that many times mass appeal comes through the silence on controversial issues; Dr. Hill consistently took a definitive stand on every major social issue in society during his lifetime, and still remained widely respected.

Run for Office

Here am I. Send me.

—ISAIAH 6:8, NIV

Too many people become comfortable with placing their hopes and dreams in the actions of others, while failing to step up to the challenges themselves. It is very easy to play Monday morning quarterback and critique what others should or should not have done, while comfortably standing on the sidelines. I firmly believe that some of the best and brightest people who have the gifts and abilities to best represent the masses need to step up to the plate and get involved.

Many of the great leaders in the history of our nation were not people of affluence or people who possessed an exceptional intellectual capacity, but rather were common men and women who had practical answers for serious challenges in our society. In America, outside of citizenship, age, and residency requirements, there are no other preconditions for representing the people. In other words, who better to represent and advocate for the needs in your community than you.

In the African American community there has been a long tradition of political and social leaders coming from the church. The church has consistently been an institution of social and spiritual renewal, and in the future things should not change. Courage is the ability to not just diagnose a problem, but to make yourself part of the solution.

Organize a Current Affairs or Political Affairs Ministry

I urge, then, first of all, that petitions, prayers, intercession and thanksgiving be made for all people—for kings and all those in authority, that we may live peaceful and quiet lives in all godliness and holiness.

—1 TIMOTHY 2:1–2, NIV

This passage highlights the important role that political and social leaders have in creating a peaceable, just, civil, and morally sound society. Some have been of the assumption that God in His divine providence would create a just society; so whatever happens or whatever policies were enacted were purely a matter of God's divine will, so Christians need not involve themselves in political or social affairs. But this passage, as well as several others, highlights the important role that not only spiritual but secular leaders have in our society, and that the role of church is to be informed and active in assisting that process to help make our society strong and vibrant. In doing so, I suggest churches and communities adopt a current affairs or public affairs ministry to educate on various policy initiatives and to provide ways of getting involved in the political and social decision making process.

This auxiliary ministry will keep church leadership and the congregants informed about significant legislation that is being proposed that will have an impact on the community. This ministry will be a vehicle for churches to draft position papers, speak at legislative hearings, and take a position on salient issues in the community. This ministry could facilitate churches hosting debates or having candidate nights. In addition the church could serve as a polling location or assist voters in getting to the polls on Election Day.

While I am not suggesting that the church become a campaign headquarters, I am suggesting that the church become very active in the decision making process in the community and consistently keep the congregants and the public informed about issues that could have a major impact on their day-to-day lives.

In our current political climate, candidates understand that if there is any hope of getting African American support on Election Day, they have to pay a visit to the church. Unfortunately what tends to happen is that candidates will attempt to draw support from congregants, who are socially and politically uninformed, via enticing words and charisma. Candidates may have positions that are contrary to the beliefs of the congregants yet they get massive support due to their charm and charisma, as opposed to the content of their message.

Seek Out and Encourage Financial Literacy

Education and slavery are incompatible.[1]

—FREDERICK DOUGLASS

Most of the political and social challenges in our country come down to issues of economics. More specifically, how will the needs of the middle and lower income effectively be addressed? In Question 3 of this study we systematically analyzed various responses to this question, with the final perspective being on self-accountability. One of the greatest challenges that exists in our culture is a deficit of financial literacy, or a basic understanding of economics on a personal and public level. Before there can ever be financial or economic justice, there must first be economic literacy. As discussed in Question 3, the causes of financial illiteracy or incompetence ranged from ignorance as to what the Bible has to say about economics or whether it was important biblically to placing political and social empowerment ahead of financial empowerment for many decades. This led to many people living a spiritually sound and holy life or intellectually sound and highly educated life, yet sinking in economic troubles that could have been avoided.

What I am encouraging is for individuals to seek out sound training and understanding of finances, economics, and money, and make this a priority! Our parents, educational institutions, and churches need to do a better job of training on personal finances and credit to young people so that they are well prepared to address the challenges in the future. Many students are graduating from colleges sinking in debt via credit cards and student loans and are unable to find a job in the area that they are passionate about because it possibly may not pay enough to support their financial obligations that they have accumulated at a young age. Some have resided in poverty for years because they never knew that there was a way out or that God was concerned about their economic well-being. Financial literacy is not just about being disciplined, but it is also about making smart decisions and/or investments. It is possible to be disciplined yet illiterate; financial literacy addresses both.

It was the great abolitionist Frederick Douglass reflecting on his time in slavery, his desire to learn how to read, and the challenges that he had as a slave trying to become literate when he stated, "education and slavery are incompatible." In other words, it is impossible to remain bound when one has access to the tools to loose themselves from the bands of what enslaves them. So in the spirit of Frederick Douglass, I argue that the key to addressing many of the challenges in the African American community, which are primarily rooted in economics, is encapsulated in financial literacy, understanding how systems work, understanding what decisions should be made, and being consistent.

NOTES

QUESTION 1

1. "Much Hope, Modest Change for Democrats: Religion in the 2008 Presidential Election," The Pew Forum on Religion and Public Life. A Project of the Pew Research Center, August 11, 2010, http://www.pewforum.org/Politics-and -Elections/Much-Hope-Modest-Change-for-Democrats-Religion-in-the-2008 -Presidential-Election.aspx (accessed July 13, 2012); information gathered from the "U.S. Religion Landscape Survey," The PEW Forum on Religion and Public Life, http://religions.pewforum.org/ (accessed July 13, 2012).

2. Ibid.

3. Barack Obama, "A More Perfect Union," (speech, National Constitution Center, Philadelphia, PA, March 18, 2008).

4. Ibid.

5. "California's Proposition 8: What Happened, and What Does the Future Hold?" National Gay and Lesbian Task Force Policy Institute, January 2009. http://www.thetaskforce.org/downloads/issues/egan_sherril_prop8_1_6_09.pdf (accessed August 1, 2012). In addition, there was a series of confrontations in California that was broadcast over the news between Gays and Blacks based upon the passage of this measure.

6. I am placing theology in two broad categories: Liberal and Conservative Theology. These labels are based largely on issues surrounding how Scripture is interpreted, belief in the inerrancy of Scripture (textual criticism), superiority of Scripture to other belief systems, significance placed on the humanity and deity of Christ, and universal authenticity of Scripture. While there are indeed differences between Evangelicals and Fundamentalists, for the purposes of this study I consider both to be Conservative. While there are indeed differences between Liberal and Neoorthodox theologies, for the purposes of this study I consider both to be more Liberal. In terms of beliefs on the issues stated above, most Protestant belief systems lean in one of the two directions.

7. *Evangelical Dictionary of Theology*, 1984 ed., ed. Walter Elwell (Grand Rapids, MI: Baker House, 1992), s.v. "Protestantism."

8. "Historic Documents of American Presbyterianism: The Doctrinal Deliverance of 1910," PCA Historical Center: Archives and Manuscript Repository for the Continuing Presbyterian Church, http://www.pcahistory.org/ documents/deliverance.html (accessed July 14, 2012).

9. Matthew 1:18–25, *The Master Study Bible, Authorized King James Version* (Nashville, TN: Cornerstone Bible Publishers, 2001).

10. Ibid., Luke 23:420–43.

11. Ibid., John 14:2.

12. Ibid., 1 Corinthians 15:19.

13. Ibid., Micah 6:8.

14. Richard J. Coleman, *Issues of Theological Conflict* (Grand Rapids, MI: Eerdmans, 1972), 106.

15. Henry P. Van Dusen, *The Vindication of Liberal Theology: A Tract for the Times* (New York: Charles Scribner's Sons, 1963), 30–31.

16. Ibid., 27.

17. *Evangelical Dictionary of Theology*, s.v. "higher criticism."

18. Van Dusen, 36.

19. Deane William Ferm, *Contemporary American Theologies: A Critical Survey* (New York: Seabury Press, 1981), 5.

20. Peter C. Hodgson and Robert H. King, *Christian Theology: An Introduction to Its Traditions and Tasks* (Philadelphia: Fortress Press, 1985), 198.

21. Van Dusen, 108.

22. Walter Rauschenbusch, *Christianity and the Social Crisis in the 21st Century: The Classic that Woke Up the Church* (New York: HarperOne, 2007), xxi.

23. Walter Rauschenbusch, *A Theology for the Social Gospel* (1917; Louisville, KY: Westminster John Knox Press, 1997), 167.

24. Ibid.

25. Ibid., 184.

26. Ibid., 36.

27. Ibid., 32–33.

28. Ibid., 40–43.

29. Ibid., 60.

30. Ibid., 148–150.

31. Ibid., 60.

32. Ibid., 9.

33. I use this term to express a time period in American history defined by sex liberation, women's liberation, Black liberation, and several other social changes in America that were focused on creating a *socially liberal culture in America*.

34. "A Conversation with James Cone: Trinity Institute's Bob Scott talks with theologian James Cone about Race, religion and violence," Trinity Wall Street. Retrieved from http://www.youtube.com/watch?v=-1X5sZ6Q4Fw (accessed August 14, 2012).

35. James Cone, *Black Theology and Black Power* (1969; Maryknoll, New York: Orbis Books, 1997), 33.

36. Ibid.

37. Ibid.

38. James Cone, *A Black Theology of Liberation: Twentieth Anniversary Edition* (1970; Maryknoll, New York: Orbis Books, 1990), 1.

39. Ibid., 2.

40. Ibid., 7.

41. Ibid., 8

42. Ibid., 6.

43. Ibid., 4.

44. Ibid.

45. Ibid., 7.

46. Ibid.

47. Ibid., 3–4; Cone, *Black Theology and Black Power*, 121–127.

48. Ibid. 120.

49. Ibid.

50. Cone, *A Black Theology of Liberation*, 120.

51. Ibid.

52. Ibid., 121.

53. Ibid., 123.

54. "How People of Faith Voted in the 2008 Presidential Race," The Barna Group, http://www.barna.org/culture-articles/18-how-people-of-faith-voted-in-the-2008-presidential-race (accessed July 14, 2012); I feel comfortable in using Christian and non-Christian interchangeably with Conservative Theology and Liberal Theology, because Conservative theologians openly accept the label as Christians, where as many Liberal Theologians hold the belief that there is a continuity between Christians and non-Christians and share many of the same perspectives on the Bible as non-Christians.

55. "Partisan Polarization Surges in Bush, Obama Years: Trends in American Values: 1987–2012," Pew Research Center, http://www.people-press.org/2012/06/04/partisan-polarization-surges-in-bush-obama-years/ (accessed July 14, 2012).

56. "Religion & Public Life: A Faith-Based Partisan Divide," The Pew Forum on Religion & Public Life, http://www.pewforum.org/uploadedfiles/Topics/Issues/Politics_and_Elections/religion-and-politics-report.pdf (accessed July 14, 2012), 2.

57. "How People of Faith Voted in the 2008 Presidential Race."

58. Mark Noll, *God and Race in American Politics: A Short History* (Princeton: Princeton University Press, 2008), 122.

59. Newport, Frank, "Religious Intensity Remains Powerful Predictor of Politics," Gallup Politics, http://www.gallup.com/poll/124649/Religious-Intensity-Remains-Powerful-Predictor-Politics.aspx (accessed July 14, 2012).

60. "A Religious Portrait of African-Americans," Pew Forum on Religion & Public Life, http://pewforum.org/A-Religious-Portrait-of-African-Americans .aspx (accessed July 14, 2012).

61. Ibid. Ibid.

62. Ibid.

63. Ibid.

64. "Religion & Public Life: A Faith-Based Partisan Divide," 4.

65. "National Organization of Women," http://www.now.org/about.html (accessed July 14, 2012).

66. Barry Goldwater, *The Conscience of a Conservative* (1969; New York: Princeton University Press, 2007), 26.

67. Ibid.

QUESTION 2

1. Pastor Robert Jeffries, Introduction of Rick Perry at the Values Voter Summit, September 7, 2011.

2. "Public Opinion n Black and White: The More Things Change the More They Stay the Same," Docstoc, http://www.docstoc.com/docs/30768692/Public -Opinion-in-Black-and-White (accessed July 15, 2012).

3. Ibid., 11.

4. Ibid., 10.

5. Cornel West, *Race Matters* (1993; New York: Vintage, 2001), 42.

6. Ibid., 43.

7. Ibid., 38–39.

8. Ibid., 43.

9. Ibid., 39.

10. Ibid.

11. Ibid., 23.

12. Ibid., 24.

13. Ibid., 25.

14. "One in 100: Behind Bars in America 2008," The Pew Center on the States, http://www.pewstates.org/uploadedFiles/PCS_Assets/2008/one%20 in%20100.pdf (accessed August 1, 2012).

QUESTION 3

1. Matthew 25:42–45, *The Master Study Bible*.

2. Matthew 26:11, NIV.

3. Deuteronomy 15:11, NIV.

4. Martin Gilens, *Why Americans Hate Welfare* (Chicago: The University of Chicago Press, 1999).

5. Ibid., 113.

6. Ibid., 114.

7. Ibid., 133–153.

8. Ibid., 125–127.

9. "Highlights," United States Census Bureau, http://www.census.gov/hhes/www/poverty/about/overview/index.html (accessed July 15, 2012).

10. Carmen DeNavas-Walt, Bernadette D. Proctor, and Jessica C. Smith, "Income, Poverty and Health Insurance Coverage in the United States: 2009," 15, US Census Bureau, http://www.census.gov/prod/2010pubs/p60-238.pdf (accessed July 15, 2012).

11. Ibid., 14.

12. Obedience to God meant following the over 600 laws that God gave to Moses in the Old Testament for the children of Israel.

13. Rauschenbusch, *Christianity and the Social Crisis in the 21st Century,* 9.

14. John C. Rodrigue, "The Freedmen's Bureau and Wage labor in the Louisiana Sugar Region," in *The Freedmen's Bureaus and Reconstruction: Reconsiderations,* ed. Paul A Cimbala and Randall M Miller, (New York: Fordham University Press, 1999), 191–195.

15. Freedmen's Bureau Bill, sec 4., March 3, 1865, *The Online Library of Liberty,* http://oll.libertyfund.org/?option=com_staticxt&staticfile=show.php%3Ftitle=2282&chapter=216250&layout=html&Itemid=27 (accessed July 15, 2012).

16. E. Allen Richardson, "Architects of a Benevolent Empire: The Relationship between the American Missionary Association and the Freedmen's Bureau in Virginia, 1865–1872," in *The Freedmen's Bureaus and Reconstruction: Reconsiderations,* 119.

17. Ibid., 124.

18. Hans L. Trefousse, "Andrew Johnson and the Freedmen's Bureau, "in *The Freedmen's Bureaus and Reconstruction: Reconsiderations,* 30–35.

19. Ibid., 32–42.

20. Mark Skousen, *The Big Three in Economics: Adam Smith, Karl Marx, and John Maynard Keynes* (Armonk, New York: M.E. Sharpe, 2007), 150.

21. Ibid.

22. John Maynard Keynes, "From Keynes to Roosevelt," *New York Times,* Sunday, December 31, 1933, 2xx. Keynes outlines his belief in an open letter to the president, which was printed in the *New York Times.*

23. "Number of the Week: Half of U.S. Lives Getting Benefits," Real Time Economics, Wall Street Journal, http://blogs.wsj.com/economics/2012/05/26/number-of-the-week-half-of-u-s-lives-in-household-getting-benefits/ (accessed July 15, 2012).

24. Congressional Budget Office, "Is Social Security Progressive?" Economic and Budget Issue Brief, December 15, 2006, http://www.cbo.gov/sites/

default/files/cbofiles/ftpdocs/77xx/doc7705/12-15-progressivity-ss.pdf (accessed July 15, 2012).

25. This statement is supported by comparing the government outlays of some of the largest social insurance programs (Social Security and Medicare) with the outlay of some of the largest means-tested programs. The data is gathered from budget data from the Congressional Budget Office, the Government Accountability Office, Office of Management and Budget, and Federal agencies' budget data looking at actual outlays from fiscal year 2011, which was not available until fiscal year 2012, and in some instances fiscal year 2013's budget proposal which contained FY 2011 actuals. The categories listed do not represent the entire list of Social Insurance or means-tested programs.

26. "Citizen's Guide to The 2011 Financial Report of The United States Government," http://www.gao.gov/financial/fy2011/11guide.pdf (accessed July 15, 2012).

27. Congressional Budget Office, "An Overview of the Supplemental Nutrition Assistance Program," http://www.cbo.gov/publication/43175; USDA, "Budget Summary and Annual Performance Plan," http://www.obpa.usda.gov/budsum/FY13budsum.pdf (accessed July 15, 2012).

28. "Social Security Administration FY 2013 President's Budget," http://www.ssa.gov/budget/2013KeyTables.pdf; DHHS, "Advancing the Health, Safety, and Well-Being of Our People: FY 2011 President's Budget for HHS," http://dhhs.gov/asfr/ob/docbudget/2011budgetinbrief.pdf (accessed July 11, 2012).

29. "Social Security Administration FY 2013 President's Budget," (these figures are for Retirement and Disability Insurance benefits and not for Supplemental Security Income which comes out of General treasury funds) Social Security's total line-item includes both Social Insurance spending and means-tested programs.

30. Ibid.; CBO, "March 2012 Medicare Benefits," http://www.cbo.gov/sites/default/files/cbofiles/attachments/43060_Medicare.pdf (accessed July 12, 2012); "Advancing the Health, Safety, and Well-Being of Our People: FY 2011 President's Budget for HHS."

31. Gareth Davies, *From Opportunity to Entitlement: The Transformation and Decline of Great Society Liberalism* (Lawrence, Kansas: The University Press of Kansas, 1996), 2–3.

32. Ibid.

33. Ibid.

34. Ibid.

35. Ibid.

36. Ibid.

37. Ibid., 45.

38. Later calculations revealed that the total cost of the bill was higher than $787 billion, but this was the original amount of the bill.

39. "Obama's Remarks on Signing the Stimulus Bill," CNN Politics, February 17, 2009, http://articles.cnn.com/2009-02-17/politics/obama.stimulus.remarks_1_economic-stimulus-bill-sign-today-speaker-pelosi?_s=PM:POLITICS (accessed July 15, 2012).

40. *American Recovery and Reinvestment Act of 2009*, HR 1, 11th Cong., 1st sess., http://frwebgate.access.gpo.gov/cgi-bin/getdoc.cgi?dbname=111_cong_bills&docid=f:h1enr.pdf (accessed July 15, 2012).

41. Barack Obama, "Year Anniversary of the Stimulus" (Speech, White-house, Washington, DC, February 17, 2010.)

42. Bureau of Labor Statistics, April 13, 2011, "Databases, Tables, & Calculators by Subject: Labor Force Statistics from the Current Population Survey," http://data.bls.gov/timeseries/LNS14000000 (accessed July15, 2012).

43. The 8 percent promise was made in a document produced by the Council of Economic Affairs, in the Office of the Vice-President Elect in early 2009 written by Christina Romer and Jared Bernstein, "The Job Impact of the American Reinvestment and Recovery Plan," January 9, 2009, 4.

44. David J. Lynch, "Economist Agree: Stimulus Created Nearly 3 Million Jobs," *USA Today*, August 30, 2010, http://www.usatoday.com/money/economy/2010-08-30-stimulus30_CV_N.htm (accessed July 15, 2012).

45. Provisions of the Affordable Care Act, HealthCare.gov, http://www.healthcare.gov/law/provisions/index.html (accessed July 15, 2012).

46. Ibid.; *National Federation of Independent Business et al. vs. Kathleen Sebelius, Secretary of Health and Human Services et al*, 567 US _____ (2012). As of date of publication of this book, the case was not yet assigned a full citation.

47. Letter from the Congressional Budget Office to House Speaker Nancy Pelosi, March 20, 2010.

48. This argument has been articulated strongest by media commentator Tavis Smiley and Professor Cornel West over the past two years. During this time they have gone around the country on a Poverty Tour and have been very critical of President Obama's economic record on poverty.

49. Adam Smith, *The Wealth of Nations* (New York: The Modern Library, 2000), 484–485.

50. Adam Smith, *The Theory of Moral Sentiments* (Amherst, New York: Prometheus Books, 2000), 122–123.

51. Smith, *The Wealth of Nations*, 15.

52. Ibid., 24.

53. Ibid., 78–79.

54. Ibid., 90.

55. Milton Friedman, *Capitalism and Freedom* (1962; Chicago: University of Chicago Press, 2002), 22–23.

56. Ibid., 8.

57. Ibid., 9.

58. Ibid., 191–192.

59. Ibid., 193. The book was written in the early '60s, so his paradigm was based from that vantage point.

60. Ibid., 193–194.

61. Ronald Reagan, "Remarks at the Signing on Signing the Tax Reform Act of 1986: October 22, 1986," http://www.reagan.utexas.edu/archives/speeches/1986/102286a.htm (accessed July 15, 2012). The comment was made in regards to the entire policy, of which Earned Income Tax Credits were a part.

62. Richard Armey and Matt Kibbe, *Give Us Liberty: A Tea Party Manifesto* (New York: Harper Luxe, 2010).

63. "Taxpayer Protection Pledge for United States House of Representative Candidates," Americans for Tax Reform, http://www.atr.org/userfiles/Congressional_pledge(1).pdf (accessed July 15, 2012).

64. "Poverty and Welfare: Highlights of the Libertarian Party's 'Ending the Welfare State Proposal,'" The Libertarian Party Issues, The Party of Principle, http://www.lp.org/issues/poverty-and-welfare (accessed July 15, 2012).

65. *Personal Responsibility and Work Opportunity Reconciliation Act*, Public Law 104–193 Title 1, §101.

66. Refer to "The Dynamic of Shifting Theological Priorities (Ideologies)."

67. Ibid.

68. Friedman defines technical monopolies as those that exist because it is efficient to have a single producer, such as railroads (*Capitalism and Freedom*, 111–112).

69. Sam Barr, "Rand Paul: Against the Civil Rights Act," http://hpronline.org/online-only/hprgument-blog/rand-paul-against-the-civil-rights-act/ (accessed July 15, 2012).

70. Comments made by Mitt Romney on *CNN*, Wednesday February 1, 2012, following the Florida Primary.

71. The Budget Battle; Countdown to Crisis: Reaching a 1991 Budget Agreement," *New York Times*, October 9, 1990, http://www.nytimes.com/1990/10/09/us/the-budget-battle-countdown-to-crisis-reaching-a-1991-budget-agreement.html (accessed July 15, 2012); "George H. W. Bush," *American Experience*, DVD, PBS Home Video, 2008.

72. "Samuel Chapman Armstrong," Hampton University, http://www.hamptonu.edu/about/armstrong.cfm (accessed July 15, 2012).

73. Ibid.

74. Booker T Washington, *Up From Slavery*, (1901; New York: Barnes and Noble, 2004), 86.

75. Ibid.

76. Ibid., 89–90.

77. Ibid., 77.

78. "A Portrait of Low Income Young Adults in Education," The Portrait Series, The Institute for Higher Education Policy, 1, http://www.ihep.org/assets/files/publications/m-r/(Brief)_A_Portrait_of_Low-Income_Young_Adults_in_Education.pdf (accessed July 15, 2012).

QUESTION 4

1. Website of Harvey Milk High School, http://www.hmi.org/ (accessed July 16, 2012).

2. Linda de Haan and Stern Nijland, *King and King* (Berkeley, CA: Tricycle Press, 2002).

3. David Parker v. William Hurley, C.A. No. 06 – 10751-MLW, United States District Court District of Massachusetts. http://www.massresistance.org/docs/parker_lawsuit/motion_to_dismiss_2007/order_motion_to_dismiss_022307.pdf (accessed July 16, 2012).

4. Mary Frances Schjonberg, "Openness of Ordination Process Affirmed," *Episcopal Life Weekly*, http://archive.episcopalchurch.org/documents/eLife_insert_081609_eng_bw_halfletter.pdf (accessed July 16 2012).

5. Ibid.

6. Defense of Marriage Act, Public Law 104-199 §7,:http://frwebgate.access.gpo.gov/cgi-bin/getdoc.cgi?dbname=104_cong_public_laws&docid=f:publ199.104 (accessed July 16, 2012); Peter Baker, "Powell Favors Repeal of Don't Ask, Don't Tell," *The New York Times*: Politics, February 3, 2010, http://thecaucus.blogs.nytimes.com/2010/02/03/powell-favors-repeal-of-dont-ask-dont-tell/?src=twt&twt=thecaucus (accessed July 16, 2012).

7. Dan Farber, "Bill Clinton: Colin Powell, Don't Ask, Don't Tell Policy Fell Short," *CBS News*: Political Hot Seat, September 21, 2010, http://www.cbsnews.com/8301-503544_162-20017186-503544.html (accessed July 16, 2012).

8. The difference between the policies were President Clinton's bill, the Defense of Marriage Act, did not seek a constitutional amendment but rather established a policy that, in terms of federal law, defined marriage as one man and one woman yet states had the flexibility to do as they pleased. One state did not have to honor the laws of another state on the issue.

9. Bill Clinton Interview with Anderson Cooper, *CNN*, 9/25/2009, http://ac360.blogs.cnn.com/2009/09/25/video-clinton-shifts-on-gay-marriage/ (accessed July 16, 2012).

10. "Statement of the Attorney General on the Litigation Involving the Defense of Marriage Act," February 23, 2011, Department of Justice, Office of Public Affairs. http://www.justice.gov/opa/pr/2011/February/11-ag-222.html (accessed July 16, 2012).

11. The narrative that will be presented primarily comes from combining events as recorded from two sources: Martin Duberman, *Stonewall* (New York: Plume, 1994) and (Kate Davis and David Heilbroner, "Stonewall Uprising," *American Experience*, DVD, PBS Video, 2010).

12. His narrative was taken from Robert Epstein, *The Times of Harvey Milk*, Documentary DVD, Image Entertainment, 2011, originally released in 1984.

13. National Organization for Women, http://www.now.org/about.html (accessed July 16, 2012).

14. Jonathan Katz, *Gay American History: Lesbians and Gay Men in the U.S.A.*, rev. ed. (New York: Meridian, 1992).

15. Michael Joseph Gross, "Gay is the New Black," Advocate.com. http://www.advocate.com/news/2008/11/16/gay-new-black (accessed July 16, 2012).

16. "Gay marriage: NAACP chairman Julian Bond says gay rights are civil rights," Monday December 7, 2009, NJ.com, http://blog.nj.com/njv_guest_blog/2009/12/gay_marriage_naacp_chairman_ju.html (accessed July 16, 2012).

17. Ronald Bayer, *Homosexuality and American Psychiatry: The Politics of Diagnosis* (Princeton, NJ: Princeton University Press, 1987).

18. "Report of the American Psychological Association Task Force on Appropriate Therapeutic Responses to Sexual Orientation," Report of the American Psychological Association Task Force on Appropriate Therapeutic Responses to Sexual Orientation, American Psychological Association, August, 2009, 23–25, http://www.apa.org/pi/lgbt/resources/therapeutic-response.pdf (accessed July 16, 2012).

19. "Answers to Your Questions for a Better Understanding of Sexual Orientation and Homosexuality," The American Psychological Association, 2008, 3, http://www.apa.org/topics/sexuality/sorientation.pdf (accessed July 16, 2012).

20. Ibid., 3–4.

21. "Report of the American Psychological Association Task Force on Appropriate Therapeutic Responses to Sexual Orientation."

22. The following sources were used to support this assertion: Duberman, *Stonewall*; Davis and Heilbroner, *Stonewall Uprising*; Epstein, *The Times of Harvey Milk*; Documentary DVD, (Image Entertainment 2011, originally released in 1984); John Scagliotti, Robert Rosenberg, Greta Schiller, *Before Stonewall*, VHS, First Run Features, 1985; John Scagliotti and Melissa Etheridge, *After Stonewall*, DVD, First Run Features, 1999; New York School Crowns Gay Couple Prom King and Queen, *Fox News*, http://www.foxnews

.com/us/2010/06/09/ny-school-crowns-gay-couple-prom-king-queen/ (accessed July 16, 2012).

23. Ibid.

24. Ibid.

25. Ibid.

26. Ibid.

27. "Spiritual Profile of Homosexual Adults Provides Surprising Profiles," The Barna Group 2009, http://www.barna.org/barna-update/article/ 13-culture/282-spiritual-profile-of-homosexual-adults-provides-surprising -insights?q=gays+christians (accessed July 16, 2012).

28. Ibid.

29. Refer to "Biblically and Racially Definitive and Indifferent Issues," Chapter 1.

30. William Stacy Johnson, *A Time to Embrace: Same Gender Relation-ships in Religion, Law and Politics* (Grand Rapids, MI: Eerdmans, 2006); Robert A. J. Gagnon and Dan O. Via, *Homosexuality and the Bible: Two Views*, (Minneapolis: Fortress Press, 2003).

31. Johnson, *A Time to Embrace*, 49.

32. Ibid., 55–57.

33. Gagnon and Via.

34. Ibid., 46.

35. Ibid.

36. Ibid., 44–45.

37. Ibid.

38. The book and the article are referenced in Byrne Fone, *Homophobia* (New York: Metropolitan, 2000), 5.

39. William Stacy Johnson offers seven theological perspectives on how to treat homosexuality. I use his general format in outlining various perspec-tives, but I condense them into three and adjust them a bit in illustrating their applicability not only in church but also in government (Johnson, *A Time to Embrace*, 40).

QUESTION 5

1. All Information about this case is retrieved from the Grand Jury Report. Court of Common Please, First Judicial District of Pennsylvania Criminal Trial Division, In RE County Investigating, Grand Jury XXIII, Misc NO 0009901-2008 c-17, Seth Williams, District Attorney, http://www.phila.gov/ districtattorney/PDFs/GrandJuryWomensMedical.pdf (accessed July 16, 2012).

2. Indirectly, this is the conclusion that the Grand Jury came to in their report.

3. Norma McCorvey and Andy Meisler, *I am ROE: My Life, Roe v Wade, and Freedom of Choice* (New York: HarperCollins, 1994), 29.

4. Ibid., 25.

5. Ibid., 47–54.

6. Ibid., 70–72.

7. Ibid., 87, 89–90.

8. Ibid., 85.

9. Ibid., 86.

10. Ibid., 101.

11. Ibid., 106–107.

12. Ibid., 115–118.

13. Sarah Weddington, *A Question of Choice* (New York: Penguin, 1992), 52.

14. McCorvey and Meisler, 122; Weddington, 52–53.

15. McCorvey and Meisler, 123.

16. Ibid., 126–127.

17. Ibid., 132–133.

18. Ibid., 126; Weddington, 62.

19. McCorvey and Meisler, 127.

20. Ibid., 132–133.

21. Ibid., 137.

22. McCorvey and Meisler, 101.

23. "United States Abortion Statistics (1973–2011)," Minnesota Citizens Concerned for Life, http://www.mccl.org/Page.aspx?pid=400 (accessed July 16, 2012); "Facts on Induced Abortion in the United States, August 2011," Guttmacher Institute, http://www.guttmacher.org/pubs/fb_induced_abortion.html (accessed July 16, 2012).

24. Rachel K. Jones and Kathryn Kooistra, "Abortion Incidence and Access to Services in the United States 2008," *Perspectives on Sexual and Reproductive Health* 43, no.1 (March 2011): 43, http://www.guttmacher.org/pubs/journals/4304111.pdf (accessed July 16, 2012).

25. "State Facts about California: National Background and Context," 2011, Guttmacher Institute, http://www.guttmacher.org/pubs/sfaa/pdf/california.pdf (accessed July 16, 2012).

26. "State Data Center: National Reproductive Health Profile," Guttmacher Institute, http://www.guttmacher.org/datacenter/profiles/US.jsp (accessed July 16, 2012).

27. Ibid.

28. "Abortion Surveillance—United States 2006 (Race)," Center for Disease Control, November 27, 2009, 58(s S08); 1–35.

29. "The Limitations of U.S. Statistics on Abortions, January 1997," Guttmacher Institute., http://www.guttmacher.org/pubs/ib14.html (accessed July 16, 2012).

30. "Guttmacher Institute State Policies in Brief as of July 1, 2012: Abortion Reporting Requirements," Guttmacher Institute, http://www.guttmacher.org/statecenter/spibs/spib_ARR.pdf (accessed July 16, 2012).

31. "The Limitations of U.S. Statistics on Abortions, January 1997."

32. Ibid.

33. Roe v Wade, 410 U.S. 113 (1973), §VIII, paragraph 2, 4, 7.

34. Ibid., §IX, part A, paragraph 2–4.

35. Ibid., §IX, part B, paragraph 1.

36. Weddington, 161–162.

37. Roe v Wade, §X, paragraph 2; Ibid, §XI.

38. Refer to Chapter 1, "Dynamic of Shifting Theological Priorities (Ideologies)."

39. "Support for Abortion Slips: Issue Ranks Lower on the Agenda," October 1, 2009, Pew Research Center, http://people-press.org/2009/10/01/support-for-abortion-slips/2/ (accessed July 16, 2012).

40. Ibid.

41. David A. Bositis, "National Opinion Poll," October 21, 2008, Joint Center for Political and Economic Studies, 11.

42. Ibid.

43. While there is some debate as to whether Margaret Sanger actually made the comment, the statement has been commonly ascribed to her.

44. Margaret Sanger and Kathryn Cullen-DuPont, *Margaret Sanger: An Autobiography,* (New York: Cooper Square Press, 1999), 20–23.

45. Ibid., 28.

46. Ibid., 45.

47. Ibid., 85–96.

48. Ibid., 106–110.

49. Ibid., 120.

50. Ibid., 103–104, 125–132.

51. Ibid., 125.

52. Linda Gordon, *The Moral Property of Women: A History of Birth Control Politics in America,* 3rd ed. (Chicago: University of Illinois Press, 2002), 39–41.

53. Ibid.

54. Sanger and Cullen-DuPont, 126–128.

55. Gordon, 41–42; Sanger and Cullen-DuPont, 128.

56. David M. Kennedy, *Birth Control in America: The Career of Margaret Sanger* (New Haven, CT: Yale University Press, 1971), 109–110; Gordon, 145.

57. Edwin Black, *War Against the Weak: Eugenics and America's Campaign to Create a Master Race* (New York: Four Walls Eight Windows, 2003), 18.

58. Ibid., 15.

59. Ibid., 17, 12.

60. Ibid., 17–18.

61. Black, 18.

62. Gordon, 87.

63. Ibid.

64. Ibid., 46.

65. Black, 22. In addition, much of Margaret Sanger's writings detail negative attitudes about the disabled who she frequently labeled as feebleminded.

66. Buck v. Bell, 274 U.S. 200 (1927).

67. Black, 32, 53.

68. Ibid., 53.

69. Ibid., 58.

70. Margaret Sanger, *The Pivot of Civilization* (eBook, Project Gutenberg, 2008), chap. IV, par. 1, http://www.gutenberg.org/dirs/1/6/8/1689/1689.txt (accessed July 16, 2012).

71. Ibid., last paragraph same chapter.

72. Margaret Sanger, "The Eugenic Value of Birth Control Propaganda," *The Birth Control Review* V, no. 10. (October 1921): 5, http://www.nyu.edu/projects/sanger/webedition/app/documents/show.php?sangerDoc=238946.xml (accessed July 16, 2012).

73. Margaret Sanger, "The Function of Sterilization: Part of An Address Delivered by Margaret Sanger before the Institute of Euthenics at Vassal College Aug 5th," *Birth Control Review* X, no. 10 (October 1926): 299, http://www.nyu.edu/projects/sanger/webedition/app/documents/show.php?sangerDoc=304387.xml (accessed July 16, 2012).

74. Gordon, 198, 203.

75. Sanger and Cullen-DuPont, 366–377.

76. Lothrop Stoddard, *The Rising Tide of Color Against White World Supremacy* (New York: Charles Scribner's Sons, 1920), 4–5, http://books.google.com/books?vid=OCLC01572150&id=Nv7TeKoQuRYC&printsec=titlepage#v=onepage&q&f=false (accessed July 16, 2012).

77. Ibid., 100–101.

78. "Eugenics and Birth Control," *The Birth Control Review: Eugenics and Birth Control* IX, no. 6 (June 1925), http://library.lifedynamics.com/Birth%20Control%20Review/1925-06%20June.pdf (accessed July 16, 2012).

79. "Birth Control or Race Control? Sanger and the Negro Project #28 Fall 2001," Margaret Sanger Paper Project, http://www.nyu.edu/projects/sanger/secure/newsletter/articles/bc_or_race_control.html (accessed July 17, 2012).

80. Ibid.

81. Ibid., par. 6, letter from Margaret Sanger to Clarence Gamble, December 1939.

82. W. E. B. Du Bois, "Black Folk and Birth Control," *Birth Control Review* XVI, no. 6. (June 1932): 166, http://library.lifedynamics.com/Birth%20Control%20Review/1932-06%20June.pdf (accessed July 17, 2012).

83. "Birth Control or Race Control? Sanger and the Negro Project #28 Fall 2001," par. 6, Letter from Margaret Sanger to Clarence Gamble December 1939.

84. Du Bois.

85. Tom Davis, "A History Lesson—The Clergy Consultation Service on Abortion: 1967–1973," *Clergy Voices: The News Letter of The Planned Parenthood Federation of America Clergy Advisory Board* 10.1 (Fall 2007): 1, https://www.plannedparenthood.org/files/ClergyVoices_07.pdf (accessed July 17, 2012).

86. Ibid.

87. Tom Davis, *Sacred Work: Planned Parenthood and its Clergy Alliances* (New Brunswick, NJ: Rutgers University Press, 2006).

88. "PPFA Clergy Advisory Board's Pastoral Letter on Abortion," *Clergy Voices: the News Letter of the Planned Parenthood Federation of America Clergy Advisory Board* 12.1, (Winter 2009), 4, http://www.plannedparenthood.org/images/PPFA/CV_Spring2009_vFinal.pdf (accessed July 17, 2012).

89. *The Master Study Bible.*

90. "Facts on Induced Abortion in the United States, August 2011," Alan Guttmacher Institute, http://www.guttmacher.org/pubs/fb_induced_abortion.html (accessed August 1, 2012).

QUESTION 6

1. "Trends in Sexually Transmitted Diseases in the United States: 2009 National Data for Gonorrhea, Chlamydia and Syphilis," Center for Disease Control, November 2010, http://www.cdc.gov/std/stats09/trends2009.pdf (accessed July 17, 2012).

2. "Sexually Transmitted Diseases: Chlamydia—CDC Fact Sheet: What Is Chlamydia?" Center for Disease Control and Prevention, http://www.cdc.gov/std/Chlamydia/STDFact-Chlamydia.htm (accessed July 17, 2012).

3. "HIV in the United States: An Overview," July 2010, Center for Disease Control, National Center for HIV/AIDS, Hepatitis, STD and TB Prevention, Division of HIV/AIDS Prevention, http://www.cdc.gov/hiv/topics/surveillance/resources/factsheets/pdf/us_overview.pdf (accessed July 17, 2012).

4. "HIV Among Gay, Bisexual and Other Men Who Have Sex With Men (MSM)," September 2010, Center for Disease Control, http://m.kpbs.org/documents/2011/jul/05/hiv-aids-numbers/ (accessed July 17 2012).

5. "HIV Among African Americans," September 2010, Center for Disease Control, http://www.cdc.gov/hiv/topics/aa/pdf/aa.pdf (accessed July 17 2012).

6. "HIV Surveillance Report: Diagnosis of HIV Infection and AIDS in the United States and Dependent Areas, 2009, Vol 21," Center for Disease Control, National Center for HIV/AIDS, Hepatitis, STD and TB Prevention, Division of HIV/AIDS Prevention, 6, http://www.cdc.gov/hiv/surveillance/resources/reports/2009report/pdf/2009SurveillanceReport.pdf (accessed July 17 2012).

7. Ibid., 9.

8. "Trends in Sexually Transmitted Diseases in the United States: 2009 National Data for Gonorrhea, Chlamydia and Syphilis."

9. Ibid.

10. Ibid.

11. "Morbidity and Mortality Weekly Report (MMWR), Summary of Notifiable Diseases-United States 2009," *Weekly*, May 13, 2011 / 58(53); 1–100, http://www.cdc.gov/mmwr/preview/mmwrhtml/mm5853a1.htm (accessed July 17 2012).

12. Ibid.

13. "Pneumocystis Pneumonia—Los Angeles," MMWR, June 5, 1981/ 30(21); 1–3, Epidemiologic Notes and Reports, Center for Disease Control, http://www.cdc.gov/mmwr/preview/mmwrhtml/june_5.htm (accessed July 17, 2012).

14. "The History of AIDS in America in the 1980s," Avert: International AIDS Charity, http://www.avert.org/aids-history-america.htm (accessed July 17, 2012).

15. Ibid.

16. Ibid.

17. Ibid.

18. "Surgeon General's Report on Acquired Immune Deficiency Syndrome," October 1986, http://profiles.nlm.nih.gov/ps/access/NNBBVN.pdf (accessed July 17, 2012).

19. "HIV Among Gay, Bisexual and Other Men Who Have Sex with Men (MSM)."

20. "Surgeon General's Report on Acquired Immune Deficiency Syndrome."

21. Thomas R. Eng and William T. Butler, eds., *The Hidden Epidemic: Confronting Sexually Transmitted Diseases* (Washington, DC: National Academic Press, 1997), 69.

22. Ibid., 74–80.

23. Ibid., 80.

24. Ibid., 92.

25. Ibid.

26. Ibid., 93.

27. A concept I introduced in Chapter 1, note 32. I use this term to express a time period in American history defined by sex liberation, women's liberation, Black liberation, and several other social changes in America that were focused on creating a socially liberal culture in America.

28. Clive Barnes, *The Report of the Commission on Obscenity and Pornography*, (New York: New York Times Book, 1970).

29. Ibid., 50, 57.

30. Richard Nixon, "Statement About the Report of the Commission on Obscenity and Pornography," October 24, 1970, http://www.presidency.ucsb.edu/ws/index.php?pid=2759#ixzz1RB9Ncn2o; John T. Woolley and Gerhard Peters, *The American Presidency Project* (Santa Barbara, CA: University of California at Santa Barbara, 1999), online at http://www.presidency.ucsb.edu/ws/?pid=2759 (accessed July 17, 2012).

31. Ibid.

32. Stanley v. Georgia, 394 U.S. 597 (1969), majority opinion final paragraph.

33. "Drug-Associated HIV Transmission Continues in the United States," Center for Disease Control, May 2002, http://www.cdc.gov/HIV/resources/factsheets/PDF/idu.pdf (accessed July 17, 2012).

34. "HIV Surveillance Report: Diagnosis of HIV Infection and AIDS in the United States and Dependent Areas, 2009, Vol 21."

35. "HIV Surveillance in Injection Drug Users," Center for Disease Control, National Center for HIV/AIDS, Hepatitis, STD and TB Prevention, Division of HIV/AIDS Prevention, http://www.cdc.gov/hiv/idu/resources/slides/slides/idu.pdf (accessed July 17, 2012).

36. "Drug-Associated HIV Transmission Continues in the United States."

37. "New CDC Analysis Reveals Strong Link Between Poverty and HIV Infection: New Study in Low Income Heterosexuals in America Inner Cities Reveals High HIV Rates," Center for Disease Control, Press Release, July 19, 2010, http://www.cdc.gov/nchhstp/newsroom/povertyandhivpressrelease.html (accessed July 17, 2012).

38. "HIV Among African Americans."

39. "National HIV/AIDS Strategy for the United States," July 2010, Presidents of the United States of America, http://www.whitehouse.gov/sites/default/files/uploads/NHAS.pdf (accessed July 17, 2012).

40. Ibid., 5.

41. Ibid., 15.

42. Ibid., 16–17.

43. Ibid., 15–16.

44. "The Title XX Adolescent Family Life Program," United States Department of Health and Human Services, Office of Population Affairs, http://www

.hhs.gov/opa/familylife/strategicplanning/overview_v6.html (accessed July 17, 2012).

45. "Personal Responsibility and Work Opportunity Act," Public Law 104–193, §912, Abstinence Education, http://frwebgate.access.gpo.gov/cgi-bin/getdoc.cgi?dbname=104_cong_public_laws&docid=f:publ193.104.pdf (accessed July 17, 2012).

46. Bowen v. Kendrick, 487 U.S. 589 (1988).

47. "Oppose Federal Funding of Abstinence-Only Education," American Civil Liberties Union, http://www.aclu.org/OPPOSE-FEDERAL-FUNDING -ABSTINENCE-ONLY-EDUCATION (accessed July 17, 2012).

48. Phyllida Burlingame, Sex Education Policy Director for the ACLU of Northern California, "ACLU: Stopping Abstinence-Only Sex Education," 07/30/2009, http://www.aclunc.org/news/aclu_on_the_radio/aclu_stopping_ abstinence-only_sex_education.shtml (accessed July 17, 2012).

49. "National Survey of Adolescents and their Parents: Attitudes and Opin- ions about Sex and Abstinence," Project No 6005, February 26, 2009, Abt Associates Inc, Cambridge Massachusetts, prepared for Family and Youth Ser- vices Bureau Administration for Children and Families, US Department of Health and Human Services, http://www.acf.hhs.gov/programs/fysb/content/ docs/20090226_abstinence.pdf (accessed July 17, 2012).

50. Ibid., IX.

51. Ibid., Xii.

52. John B. Jemmott, Loretta Jemmott, and Gregory Fong, "Efficacy of a Theory Based Abstinence-Only Intervention Over 24 Months: A Randomized Controlled Trial With Young Adults" *Archives of Pediatrics and Adolescent Medicine* 164, no. 2 (February 1, 2010): 152, http://archpedi.ama-assn.org/cgi/ reprint/164/2/152?maxtoshow=&hits=10&RESULTFORMAT=&fulltext=Ab stinence+Education&searchid=1&FIRSTINDEX=0&resourcetype=HWCIT (accessed July 17, 2012).

53. Robert Stein, "Abstinence-Only Programs Might Work, Study Says," *The Washington Post*, February 2, 2010, http://www.washingtonpost.com/ wp-dyn/content/article/2010/02/01/AR2010020102628.html (accessed July 17, 2012).

54. "Efficacy of a Theory Based Abstinence-Only Intervention Over 24 Months, 157.

55. Consolidated Appropriations Acts of 2010.H.R. 3288, http://www.gpo .gov/fdsys/pkg/BILLS-111hr3288enr/pdf/BILLS-111hr3288enr.pdf (accessed July 17, 2012).

56. "SIECUS State Profiles: Sexuality Education and Abstinence-Only-Until- Marriage Programs in the States: An Overview Fiscal Year 2010," Sexuality Information and Education Council of the United States, http://www.siecus

.org/index.cfm?fuseaction=Page.viewPage&pageId=487&parentID=478 (accessed July 17, 2012).

57. Ibid.

58. "Department of Health and Human Services, Implementation Guidance for Syringe Services Programs July 2010," Center for Disease Control, http:// www.cdc.gov/hiv/resources/guidelines/PDF/SSP-guidanceacc.pdf (accessed July 17, 2012).

59. "Determination that a Demonstration Needle Exchange Program Would be Effective in Reducing Drug Abuse and the Risk of Acquired Immune Deficiency Syndrome Infection Among Intravenous Drug Users," February 23, 2011, Federal Register, Department of Health and Human Services, http:// federalregister.gov/a/2011-3990 (accessed July 17, 2012).

60. "Reducing Drug Harm," Issues, Drug Policy Alliance, http://www .drugpolicy.org/issues/reducing-drug-harm (accessed July 17, 2012).

61. Ibid.

62. "Supervised Injection Facilities," Drug Policy Alliance, http://www .drugpolicy.org/resource/supervised-injection-facilities (accessed July 17, 2012).

63. "The Sharing of Drug Injection Equipment and the AIDS Epidemic in New York City: The First Decade," in eds. R. J. Battjesand R. W. Pickens, *Needle Sharing Among Intravenous Drug Abusers: National and International Perspectives* (Washington, D.C.: National Institute on Drug Abuse, 1988), 87–89, http://archives.drugabuse.gov/pdf/monographs/80.pdf (accessed July 17, 2012); Sondra D. Lane, "Needle Exchange: A Brief History," The AIDS Education Global Information Systems (AIEGIS) Law Library http://ww1.aegis .org/law/journals/1993/HKFNE009.html (accessed July 17, 2012).

64. Ibid.

65. Ibid.

66. Jane Gross, "Needle Exchange for Addicts Wins Foothold Against Aids in Tacoma," January 23, 1989, *New York Times*, http://www.nytimes. com/1989/01/23/us/needle-exchange-for-addicts-wins-foothold-against-aids-in -tacoma.html?src=pm (accessed July 17, 2012).

67. North American Syringe Exchange Network, www.nasen.org (accessed August 2, 2012).

68. "Needle Exchange and Harm Reduction," AVERTing HIV and AIDS, http://www.avert.org/needle-exchange.htm (accessed July 18, 2012).

69. Lane.

70. "Needle Exchange Programs: Research Suggest Promise as an AIDS Prevention Strategy," U.S. Government Accounting Office, March 1993, http:// archive.gao.gov/d44t15/148846.pdf (accessed July 18, 2012); David Vlahov and Benjamin Junge, The Role of Needle Exchange Programs in HIV Prevention," *Public Health Reports* 113, Supp. 1 (June 1998), 75–80, available at http://www

.ncbi.nlm.nih.gov/pmc/articles/PMC1307729/pdf/pubhealthrep00030-0079.pdf (accessed July 18, 2012).

71. Advocates for Youth, "Characteristics of Effective Sexuality and HIV Education Programs," Advocates for Youth, http://www.advocatesforyouth.org/topics-issues/sex-education/832?task=view (accessed July 18, 2012).

72. "Education Q&A: How Do School Based Sexuality Programs Differ?" Sexuality Information and Education Council of the United States of America, Sexuality (SIECUS), http://www.siecus.org/index.cfm?fuseaction=page.viewpage&pageid=521&grandparentID=477&parentID=514 (accessed July 18, 2012).

73. "Policy Brief, Abstinence-Only-Until-Marriage-Programs: Ineffective, Unethical and Poor Public Health," Advocates for Youth, http://www.advocatesforyouth.org/storage/advfy/documents/pbabonly.pdf (accessed July 18, 2012).

74. Gregg Brekke, "UCC's Health Advocates Press for Increased Condom Distribution," March 20, 2009, United Church of Christ News, http://www.ucc.org/news/uccs-health-advocates-press.html (accessed July 18, 2012).

QUESTION 7

1. "The Horrors of Slavery and England's Duty to Free the Bondsman: An Address Delivered in Taunton, England, on September 1, 1846, *Somerset County Gazette,* September 5, 1846, http://www.yale.edu/glc/archive/1081.htm (accessed July 18, 2012).

About the Author

CHRISTOPHER SIGNIL IS a licensed minister who has served in a wide range of ministerial assignments for most of his life. He has also worked on several campaigns and has extensive experience working in a variety of non-profit organizations. Christopher has a Bachelor of Arts in Political Science from Virginia State University, he has completed Graduate study at The John Glenn Institute at The Ohio State University in Public Administration, he has a Master's in Political Management from George Washington University, and certificate in External Studies from Valor Christian College.

CONTACT THE AUTHOR

E-mail:

csignil@gmail.com

Website:

www.racefaithandpolitics.com